CAMPAIGN • 201

BRANDY STATION 1863

First step towards Gettysburg

DAN BEATTIE

ILLUSTRATED BY ADAM HOOK

Series editors Marcus Cowper and Nikolai Bogdanovic

First published in Great Britain in 2008 by Osprey Publishing,
Midland House, West Way, Botley, Oxford OX2 0PH, UK
443 Park Avenue South, New York, NY 10016, USA
E-mail: info@ospreypublishing.com

A CIP catalog record for this book is available from the British Library.

ISBN: 978 1 84603 304 9

Editorial by Ilios Publishing Ltd, Oxford, UK (www.iliospublishing.com)
Page layout by: The Black Spot
Index by Alison Worthington
Typeset in Sabon and Myriad Pro
Maps by The Map Studio Ltd
3D bird's-eye views by The Black Spot
Battlescene illustrations by Adam Hook
Originated by PDQ Digital Media Solutions
Printed in China through Worldprint Ltd.

08 09 10 11 12   10 9 8 7 6 5 4 3 2 1

FOR A CATALOG OF ALL BOOKS PUBLISHED BY OSPREY MILITARY AND
AVIATION PLEASE CONTACT

NORTH AMERICA
Osprey Direct, c/o Random House Distribution Center, 400 Hahn Road,
Westminster, MD 21157
E-mail: info@ospreydirect.com

ALL OTHER REGIONS
Osprey Direct UK, P.O. Box 140 Wellingborough, Northants, NN8 2FA, UK
E-mail: info@ospreydirect.co.uk

www.ospreypublishing.com

ACKNOWLEDGMENTS

My wife Peggy helped me in many ways with this book. Much thanks to
Dr. Gary W. Gallagher, Clark "Bud" Hall, Joseph W. McKinney, and Robert J.
Trout for their assistance and especially for stoking the fires of my interest
in this topic. Many librarians, too many to name, offered kind help. My
editor, Marcus Cowper, was pleasant to work with and skilled at his craft.

ARTIST'S NOTE

Readers may care to note that the original paintings from which the
colour plates in this book were prepared are available for private sale.
All reproduction copyright whatsoever is retained by the Publishers.
All enquiries should be addressed to:

Scorpio Gallery, PO Box 475, Hailsham, East Sussex, UK

The Publishers regret that they can enter into no correspondence upon
this matter.

THE WOODLAND TRUST

Osprey Publishing are supporting the Woodland Trust, the UK's leading
woodland conservation charity, by funding the dedication of trees.

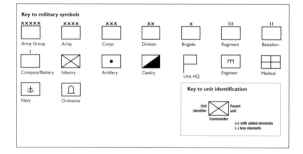

CONTENTS

The theater of war in north-central Virginia, June 1863

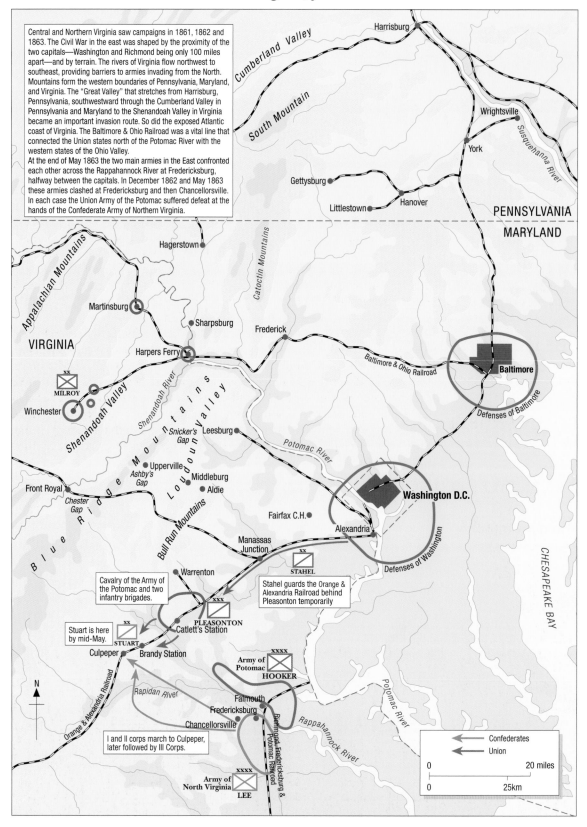

Central and Northern Virginia saw campaigns in 1861, 1862 and 1863. The Civil War in the east was shaped by the proximity of the two capitals—Washington and Richmond being only 100 miles apart—and by terrain. The rivers of Virginia flow northwest to southeast, providing barriers to armies invading from the North. Mountains form the western boundaries of Pennsylvania, Maryland, and Virginia. The "Great Valley" that stretches from Harrisburg, Pennsylvania, southwestward through the Cumberland Valley in Pennsylvania and Maryland to the Shenandoah Valley in Virginia became an important invasion route. So did the exposed Atlantic coast of Virginia. The Baltimore & Ohio Railroad was a vital line that connected the Union states north of the Potomac River with the western states of the Ohio Valley.

At the end of May 1863 the two main armies in the East confronted each other across the Rappahannock River at Fredericksburg, halfway between the capitals. In December 1862 and May 1863 these armies clashed at Fredericksburg and then Chancellorsville. In each case the Union Army of the Potomac suffered defeat at the hands of the Confederate Army of Northern Virginia.

Cumberland Valley

Harrisburg

South Mountain

Wrightsville

York

Susquehanna River

Gettysburg

Littlestown

Hanover

PENNSYLVANIA

MARYLAND

Hagerstown

Catoctin Mountains

Appalachian Mountains

Martinsburg

Sharpsburg

Frederick

VIRGINIA

Harpers Ferry

Baltimore & Ohio Railroad

Baltimore

Defenses of Baltimore

XX
MILROY

Shenandoah River

Winchester

Shenandoah Valley

Snicker's Gap

Leesburg

Loudoun Valley

Blue Ridge Mountains

Upperville

Ashby's Gap

Middleburg

Aldie

Potomac River

Front Royal

Chester Gap

Bull Run Mountains

Fairfax C.H.

Washington D.C.

Alexandria

Manassas Junction

XX
STAHEL

Defenses of Washington

CHESAPEAKE BAY

Cavalry of the Army of the Potomac and two infantry brigades.

Warrenton

Stahel guards the Orange & Alexandria Railroad behind Pleasonton temporarily

XXX
PLEASONTON

Catlett's Station

Stuart is here by mid-May.

XX
STUART

Culpeper

Brandy Station

Army of Potomac
XXXX
HOOKER

Orange & Alexandria Railroad

Rapidan River

N

Falmouth

Fredericksburg

Chancellorsville

Richmond, Fredericksburg & Potomac Railroad

Rappahannock River

Potomac River

I and II corps march to Culpeper, later followed by III Corps.

Army of North Virginia
XXXX
LEE

Confederates

Union

0   20 miles

0   25km

THE EVE OF BATTLE

Culpeper Court House had seen armies before. Pictured is a camp of part of General John Pope's invading Army of Virginia in the summer of 1862. The leftmost steeple marks the courthouse itself, where Stuart held a ball on the evening of June 4, 1863. The train depot is in the center. Note the fence stripped of its rails in the foreground. (Library of Congress)

The road to Gettysburg began at Brandy Station. But the cavalry clash in Culpeper County, Virginia, counts for more than just the opening round of Lee's second invasion of the North. The battle on June 9, 1863, showed both sides that the Union cavalry had come of age. It signaled that horsemen blue and gray were now equal in ability. It also refuted for good the snide remark of General Joseph Hooker: "Whoever saw a dead cavalryman?" It was the largest cavalry battle of the American Civil War.

War had visited Culpeper's woods, towns and rolling fields several times during the preceding two years. Armies had marched across it, camped there, sparred with each other and, in 1862, fought the battle of Cedar Mountain. In March 1863—three months before the battle of Brandy Station—a large raiding force of Union cavalry had crossed the Rappahannock River into Culpeper and attacked Confederate horsemen near Kelly's Ford. In April several corps of Union infantry and cavalry passed through the county during the Chancellorsville operations. Dismantled fences, missing livestock, ruined

Auburn plantation, the home of John Minor Botts, hosted the great cavalry reviews that Stuart staged in June 1863. (Library of Congress)

roads, embittered civilians and the fresh graves of local boys were the price Culpeper had paid so far in the Confederate war for independence. In the late spring of 1863, war came calling again.

The Confederate cavalry was ready for war that spring. In late May they left Lee's Army, massed around Fredericksburg, and made an easy two-day ride west to central Culpeper County, a region of plentiful forage and plentiful strategic opportunities. One South Carolina captain wrote home about what he saw: "Culpeper, I think, has been more severely ravaged by the Yankees than any other county I have seen. For miles and miles, the country is depopulated, fine mansions are untenanted and the fencing of the plantations are all destroyed. Yet in its desolation it is beautiful. It smiles even in its tears. The number of fields everywhere, though unfenced, are covered over with the finest clover and timothy." The commander of the Confederate cavalry, the capable and colorful James Ewell Brown ("Jeb") Stuart, soon staged several magnificent reviews. The general invited the public to the one on June 5. Nine-thousand Confederate horsemen, with fluttering standards, flashing sabers and well-groomed steeds, were on parade. "It was a brilliant day, and the thirst for the 'pomp and circumstance' of war was fully satisfied," remembered a cavalry staff officer. Stuart was in his glory. Another Confederate officer thought the last review was a sight "not soon to be forgotten. … There could be no doubt the cavalry was as ready for the work before us as was our matchless infantry." Never before were Lee's horsemen so numerous, so confident, so prepared. Not only were Stuart's men in the county, Lee's was also massing his three infantry corps there. Lee meant to carry war across the Potomac again.

A few miles east along the railroad from the review ground was the whistle stop of Brandy Station; and three miles beyond that the Rappahannock River, the northeastern border of the county and one of the great rivers of Virginia. Brandy Station had only a few, unpretentious buildings. It was no rival for prestige to the village of Stevensburg, four miles south, or the county seat, Culpeper Court House, eight miles west. The county covered 381 square miles and held about 12,000 people, mostly farmers with a few tradesmen. About half of the population were black slaves. To the east, the county was bordered by the small Rapidan River, which flowed into the Rappahannock. A tributary of the Rapidan named Crooked Run formed the southern border. The Blue Ridge Mountains—easternmost chain of the Appalachian Mountains—and hilly Rappahannock County formed the northwestern boundary of the county and separated it from the Shenandoah Valley. The main commercial artery of the county was the Orange and Alexandria Railroad. Some 60 miles along its tracks to the northeast lay Alexandria, Virginia, across the Potomac River from the Union capital. Ninety miles by rail to the southeast of Culpeper was Richmond, the Confederate capital. Thirty miles to the east was Fredericksburg, where the two great armies of the North and South in the east confronted each other across the Rappahannock in the winter and early spring of 1863.

On the evening of the last review, Stuart issued orders to his brigades to camp within a few miles of Brandy Station and the Rappahannock River crossings. They would cross the next morning to screen the advance of Lee's army. He ordered his staff to pitch the tent flies next to a white two-story, board house owned by a man named Miller, on the southern end of a prominent two-mile-long ridge a mile east of Brandy Station. As was the custom, Miller had given his home a nickname: Fleetwood. Stuart's headquarters sat on Fleetwood Hill from the evening of June 8 until the following morning.

A British officer wrote after the war: "The truth is that the Americans struck the true balance between shock and dismounted tactics. It may be unhesitatingly declared that the horseman of the American war is the model of the efficient cavalryman." This rare photo shows a complete cavalry regiment, the 13th New York Cavalry, near Washington. Note the band mounted on white horses in the rear. (Library of Congress)

Lee and Stuart review their horsemen on June 8, 1863. Behind Stuart is Major Heros von Borcke, holding on to his hat. (*Brandy Station Review*, painting by Don Troiani, www.historicalimagebank.com)

Rumors of Lee's intentions, distant artillery rumbling on June 5 and word of the "grand reviews" of the massed Southern cavalry, had reached their adversaries across the Rappahannock. General Joseph Hooker reacted. As new commander of the Army of the Potomac, Hooker had greatly improved his command in the early spring of 1863. Among other reforms, he had ordered his horsemen concentrated into a cavalry corps, the better to perform the traditional cavalry tasks of concealing their own army and finding out what Lee's army was doing. For two years under the able "Jeb" Stuart, the Confederate cavalry had performed those roles superbly, often at the expense of the Yankee horsemen.

Even before that spring, the Union cavalry had learned to ride and use their weapons. Cavalry leaders with energy and initiative had started to emerge. But by massing the Union horsemen into their own corps, about 11,000 strong, Hooker put them on a new level in the Army of the Potomac and enhanced their *esprit de corps*. Now they were eager to meet their Southern counterparts in battle. Gone now were the days, as one Yankee put it, when Union cavalry could only surrender, die or run when Stuart's men attacked. Now the horsemen in blue had been given the opportunity to be real cavalrymen. Infantry would take over many of their former chores. Hooker appointed Major-General George Stoneman commander of the new Cavalry Corps; generals Alfred Pleasonton, William Averell and David Gregg would command its divisions. Hooker and these leaders also revamped the quantity and quality of weapons and horses. Review boards weeded out poor officers; new uniforms and equipment were issued, including a cavalry corps badge; drill was regularized; even food and forage were improved a little. Medical care, for man and beast, was enhanced. Hooker also sought to reverse the often-shabby treatment Union cavalrymen gave their horses. Now Hooker possessed a force well suited for counter-reconnaissance, raiding enemy military or economic targets, even for striking a powerful blow against Stuart. Naturally, he wanted to put them to the test. Opportunities came. The cavalry failed the first challenge, however, partly because one of Hooker's reforms had yet to be implemented fully: the cavalry cordon stretching over 100 miles around the army was still in place.

On February 22, Confederate Brigadier-General Fitzhugh Lee with 400 picked Virginia cavalry penetrated the thinly held Union cavalry picket lines at Kelly's Ford on the upper Rappahannock. Rampaging in the Union rear areas, they reached Hartwood Church—a mere twelve miles from army headquarters at Falmouth, Virginia. The Confederates returned across the snow with much military loot, including 150 captured Union troopers. The raid humiliated the Union Army. Two divisions of the new Cavalry Corps went after the raiders but acted at cross-purposes and failed to catch them. "Fitz" Lee even left Averell, an old classmate from West Point and one of the generals pursuing him, an insulting note daring Averell to come south for a return "visit." Hooker was furious. He gladly approved a "visit" to "Fitz" Lee by Averell and 4,000 sabers three weeks later.

General George Stoneman was the first commander of the Cavalry Corps, Army of the Potomac. Unfortunately for a cavalryman, he was afflicted with hemorrhoids. (Library of Congress)

Though the Confederates had early warning of the Union approach, it was their turn to be surprised when Averell hurled most of his command across the Rappahannock at Kelly's Ford. A Confederate outpost contested the crossing for an hour. News of the Yankee incursion into Culpeper County drew "Fitz" Lee's gaunt brigade from its camp near the Court House. For five hours on March 17 the two sides tussled, mostly on horseback. Several times during the fight, Lee launched fierce charges upon the Yankee cavalry and horse artillery. "They came on boldly, yelling like demons, and apparently confident of victory," said a Union officer. The charges, fuelled by arrogance and a tradition of victory, did not succeed this time. Lee was outnumbered, and the blue troopers showed new confidence and skill. They were particularly adept with their sabers, and counterattacked with relish. Some Confederates shouted to the Union men to sheath their sabers and fight with pistols "like gentlemen." The Union force was about to sweep the field of the exhausted Confederates when Averell was struck by an attack of timidity and ordered a retreat. Had he been a bit more resolute, Averell might have destroyed his opponents. But the little battle of Kelly's Ford was another milestone in the growing reputation of the Union cavalry. The whole Cavalry Corps felt pride in the "whipping" that their comrades had given the Confederate cavalry on St. Patrick's Day. One Union colonel asserted: "the spirits of our men never were as good as they are now." And Hooker felt vindicated in his decision to create the new corps. Other opportunities would arrive in April 1863, after the ground dried and Virginia's roads became more usable.

As a wing commander during the bloody fiasco of the battle of Fredericksburg, "Fighting Joe" Hooker had seen first hand how strong the Confederate defenses were at that city. Now as the new campaigning season began, Hooker was in charge of a reinvigorated Army of the Potomac and had a plan to bypass Lee's position. While some of the infantry would pin Lee at Fredericksburg and draw his attention, the bulk of the army would secretly force-march from 15 to 25 miles up the Rappahannock. Once across the river, the mobile force would plant itself on Lee's flank, to the rear of the Fredericksburg lines. Hooker predicted that Lee would either have to come

This picture of a cavalry patrol represents the most important duties of cavalry: finding the location of the enemy and resisting the attempts of the enemy to find the elements of your army. (Library of Congress)

out of his defenses and fight outnumbered without a terrain advantage or "ingloriously flee." Hooker's role for his cavalry was as imaginative as his plan for the rest of the army. Stoneman would take most of his horsemen, 8,000 strong, even further upriver, cross ahead of the infantry and stir up trouble in Lee's rear. Hooker told him to smash up Hanover Junction, where two key railroads essential to supplying Lee crossed. The plan meant that Stoneman would be cut off from communication and coordination with Hooker most of the time. Only General Pleasonton and a brigade of his cavalry division would remain with Hooker and the main army.

Both the weather and lack of zeal on the part of Stoneman combined to undermine the cavalry part of Hooker's strategy. After a bold start in mid-April, Stoneman delayed crossing the upper Rappahannock into Culpeper County. Then two weeks of almost constant rain prevented a crossing. Hooker halted him; then he sent him out again with slightly different orders. Once over the river, Stoneman sent Averell's Division southward. Averell did not get far. Faced by minor Confederate opposition, he dithered along the banks of the Rapidan River, burnt a few unimportant bridges and then headed back to the cavalry camps near Falmouth from which he had started. Stoneman, meanwhile, after tarrying at Kelly's Ford for a day, led the larger part of his force—Gregg's reinforced division—southeastward, well behind Lee's Army at Fredericksburg. Astride the main line of supply between Lee and Richmond, Stoneman cut the rail line. Stoneman did not try to link up with Hooker, who by then had successfully outflanked Lee by crossing the Rappahannock west of Fredericksburg. Nor did he attack the rear of Lee's Army. Nor did he keep his column intact as a powerful striking force. Instead he followed Hooker's revised orders: to split his command into one- and two-regiment packets and strike out in all directions, acting like a bursting shell, in Stoneman's colorful simile. Ironically, in this first large-scale operation of the united cavalry of the army, Hooker and Stoneman temporarily broke up the Cavalry Corps. Before reassembling safely behind Union lines at Yorktown a week later, the Union troopers had sowed panic, damaged Confederate railroads, and ruined a considerable amount of property. Colonel Judson Kilpatrick had even brought his regiment to the gates of Richmond, gates he found heavily guarded against raiders.

When it was over, and the cost tallied, the great raid had merely alarmed the Confederates, caused damage soon repaired and wore out more than 1,000 Union cavalry horses. The cost should also include both depriving Hooker of most of his cavalry as he entered strange territory and allowing Lee's cavalry to locate and exploit the crucial weakness of the Union position at Chancellorsville. Not having much cavalry, in addition, may have helped weaken Fighting Joe's resolve when Lee and Jackson finally struck. Apparently Hooker's backbone collapsed even before a corps of his army ran away. A defeated and dispirited Union army finally retreated back across the Rappahannock, where they eventually met their worn-out cavalry. The one bit of sunshine in this latest painful disaster was that the Union cavalry had improved their morale by aggressively taking the fight into the enemy country in the largest raid ever undertaken by the army's mounted arm. Many of the cavalrymen had welcomed the danger and fatigue of a raid over the tedium and toil of camp life. Many looked forward to the next one.

During the weeks after Chancellorsville, while his army licked its wounds Hooker made changes in his cavalry. He dismissed Stoneman and Averell. Alfred Pleasonton, who had wildly exaggerated his accomplishments in the last battle—even persuading Hooker that he had saved the army—was elevated to provisional command of the Cavalry Corps. Having cleaned house, Hooker turned his attention again to Robert E. Lee. Would Lee grab the initiative before Hooker was ready to strike again?

CHRONOLOGY

1863

January 26   The Army of the Potomac gets its third commander, as Major-General Joseph Hooker replaces General Ambrose Burnside.

February 2   As part of his reforms, Hooker creates the Cavalry Corps from the various cavalry units of his army. Major-General George Stoneman is its first leader.

March 17   A major portion of the Cavalry Corps under Averell raids Culpeper County to bring "Fitz" Lee's Confederate cavalry brigade to battle at Kelly's Ford.

April 29 to May 7   In the first large-scale Union cavalry raid of the war, Stoneman takes most of the Union cavalry deep behind Lee's Army during the Chancellorsville campaign.

April 30 to May 3   Lee defeats Hooker at Chancellorsville. Meanwhile, Stoneman accomplishes little.

May 15   Lee meets with President Davis and wins his approval for a summer campaign by Lee's army on Northern soil.

May 22   Hooker replaces Stoneman temporarily with Brigadier-General Alfred Pleasonton.

May 15 to June 15   Lee begins to move his army secretly from Fredericksburg to Culpeper County as part of a second invasion of the North.

May 22, June 5, June 8   Stuart stages three reviews of his cavalry division in Culpeper County.

June 9   Following Hooker's orders, Pleasonton crosses the Rappahannock River with most of the Cavalry Corps and attacks Stuart at Brandy Station.

June 10   Lee starts his army northward.

June 14	Ewell's Corps of Lee's army attacks and destroys a small Union army at Winchester, in the lower Shenandoah Valley.
June 17 to 21	Pleasonton attacks Stuart in the Loudoun Valley in an effort to reach the Blue Ridge gaps into the Shenandoah and locate the bulk of Lee's army. Battles of Aldie, Middleburg, and Upperville.
June 22	Pleasonton is promoted to major-general and confirmed as head of the Cavalry Corps.
June 26 to July 2	Stuart attempts with three of his brigades to ride around Hooker's army as it marches northward toward Maryland and Pennsylvania. Stuart takes a circuitous route back to the Army of Northern Virginia.
June 28	Meade replaces Hooker as commander of the Army of the Potomac.
June 30	Cavalry fight at Hanover, Pennsylvania.
July 1	Buford's cavalry division delays the Confederate capture of Gettysburg. The great battle begins.

OPPOSING PLANS

Major-General Joseph Hooker was an excellent brigade, division and corps commander. However, he was found lacking as an army leader. One of his accomplishments was to create the Cavalry Corps for his Army of the Potomac. (Library of Congress)

UNION PLANS

Hooker was convinced until the middle of June that Lee's Army still faced him at Fredericksburg. But information filtering out of Culpeper County alarmed him. Another of his administrative accomplishments had been the creation of the Bureau of Military Information (BMI), an intelligence-gathering and analysis outfit at army headquarters. Colonel George Sharp and his BMI men weighed the information coming in. There were reports from escaped slaves, Union sympathizers behind enemy lines, Confederate deserters, captured Rebels, Pleasonton's cavalry, as well as Sharp's own corps of scouts and spies. Even Southern newspapers could provide clues. Apparently the cavalry of the Army of Northern Virginia was massing in Culpeper County. Either Stuart meant another large-scale cavalry raid, or he was the vanguard of another thrust by Lee at Washington, D.C., on Northern soil. Lee also planted the rumor of a cavalry raid to distract attention from the northwestward shift of his whole army.

Much of Pleasonton's Corps was already near Culpeper: just across the Rappahannock in Fauquier County. There it guarded the Orange & Alexandria Railroad, an important secondary supply line for the Union Army, and watched for any signs of Confederates in the neighborhood. Hooker assured Lincoln that if a raid was imminent that "it was his great desire to 'bust it up' before it got fairly under way." The cavalry was the obvious tool. Not trusting the planning to newly appointed Pleasonton, Hooker prepared detailed orders. He recommended crossing simultaneously at Kelly's and Beverly fords and then advancing upon Culpeper Court House, where Stuart's cavalry probably were. Pleasonton should also send a small force to Stevensburg to keep an eye on the road from Fredericksburg. By implication, Pleasonton was to keep his eyes open for Confederate infantry marching to join Stuart. Hooker told Pleasonton that he could divide his force as he saw fit but to keep in mind his primary mission: "to disperse and destroy the rebel force assembled in the vicinity of Culpeper." He also instructed Pleasonton to pursue Stuart vigorously if he should rout him. Hooker agreed to a request from Pleasonton for some infantry "stiffening" for the Cavalry Corps. He loaned two ad hoc brigades, each with 1,500 hand-picked veteran infantry and a horse artillery battery. The infantry brigades were to be concentrated at Brandy Station once over the river and used as a "point of support," a rallying point that no enemy cavalry could break. In addition, General Meade, whose 5th Corps picket lines reached to Kelly's Ford, was told to help out in protecting the left flank of the advance. As it turned out, Meade would send a full brigade from his corps a few miles into Culpeper County to back up the cavalry.

Pleasonton then planned how to divide his force. He apparently did not question the use of two fords six miles apart when there were two others available in between them. He adhered to Hooker's admonition to be secretive. Even the infantry were cautioned to reach the river by roundabout marches. Pleasonton decided to form two wings for the crossings until the Cavalry Corps re-concentrated at Brandy Station. The Right Wing, crossing at Beverly, would be under the command of Brigadier-General John Buford, and consist of the 1st Division, the Reserve Cavalry Brigade and one of those picked infantry brigades. Sixteen guns, as well as Pleasonton himself, would accompany this wing. The Left Wing, crossing at Kelly's Ford, would be led by Brigadier-General David Gregg and consist of Colonel Alfred Duffie's 2nd Division, Gregg's own 3rd Division, the other infantry brigade and 18 guns. Each column would have about 5,500 men. From the total for the right wing, however, one should subtract about 1,500 men who would guard the north bank of the river at the ford and the line of supply and communication (and retreat) to Catlett's Station. Hooker and Pleasonton had been informed that 1,700 of Stahel's Division, assigned ordinarily to the Washington defenses, was on its way along the Orange & Alexandria Railroad to relieve Pleasonton's garrison at Catlett's Station. From the viewpoints of the army and cavalry corps commanders, everything seemed in place to get a large force across the Rappahannock at daybreak on June 9, 1863, and send it a dozen miles westward to "disperse and destroy" the Southern horsemen near Culpeper Court House.

Brigadier-General Alfred Pleasonton, new commander of the cavalry of the Army of the Potomac, was held in greater esteem by many of his superiors as well as the general public than by many of his soldiers. (Library of Congress)

CONFEDERATE PLANS

The idea for a second Confederate invasion of the North was born soon after Chancellorsville. Although Lee had won a stunning victory against high odds in the thickets of the Wilderness around Chancellorsville clearing, he had paid a high price. The South could ill afford 12,000 casualties; and the loss of Stonewall Jackson was irreparable. Lee had parried a major Union thrust, but more, perhaps stronger, blows were sure to come. Virginia had been the richest Southern state before the war. Now half of the state was behind enemy lines, her commerce greatly reduced, and many of her railroads, valuable cropland, and some of her industrial sites and chief cities lost to the Confederacy. Most threatening of all was the presence of the Army of the Potomac just 50 miles from Richmond, the capital and soul of the Confederacy. Lee knew that if he stayed on the defensive he would be ground down in a war of attrition. And if the Army of Northern Virginia was destroyed, the Confederacy was doomed.

Many advisers, including General Longstreet and several members of the Confederate cabinet, had suggested that Lee take part of the army westward to lift the siege of Vicksburg, Mississippi. General Grant's army had that city and the army within it in a death-grip. But Lee was convinced that the war could be won only in the East. "We should assume the aggressive," he told President Davis. If he took his army into the Northern states of Maryland and Pennsylvania an opportunity might arise to destroy the Army of the Potomac on its home soil. Even severely damaging Hooker's Army there might dramatically increase the clamor of the Northern Peace Democrats

General Robert E. Lee was the embodiment of a Virginia gentleman and was widely respected as a soldier. His decision to invade the North in 1863 triggered the cavalry battle of Brandy Station. (Library of Congress)

Eastern Culpeper County, Virginia, on 8 June, 1863

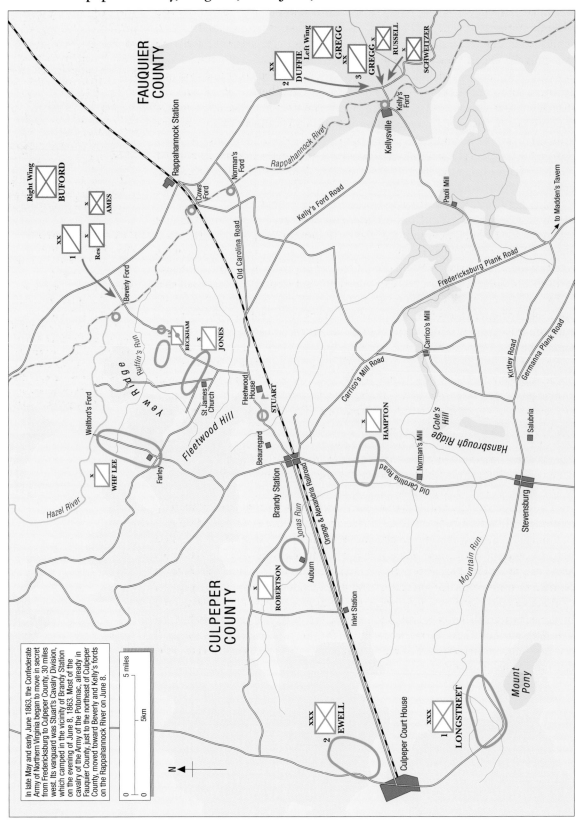

FAUQUIER COUNTY

Left Wing
DUFFIE
2
XX

GREGG
GREGG
3
XX

RUSSELL
x

SCHWEITZER
x

Kelly's Ford
Kellysville

to Madden's Tavern

Paoli Mill

Right Wing
BUFORD
XX

AMES
x

1
XX

Res
x

Rappahannock Station

Norman's Ford

Cows Ford

Rappahannock River

Kelly's Ford Road

Carrico's Mill

Fredericksburg Plank Road

Germanna Plank Road

Kirtley Road

Beverly Ford

Ruffin's Run

BECKHAM

JONES
x

St James Church

Fleetwood House

STUART

Wellford's Ford

Yew Ridge

Fleetwood Hill

Beauregard

HAMPTON
x

Cole's Hill

Norman's Mill

Hansbrough Ridge

Salubria

WHF LEE
x

Farley

Hazel River

Brandy Station

Jonas Run

Old Carolina Road

Carrico's Mill Road

Orange & Alexandria Railroad

Mountain Run

Stevensburg

ROBERTSON
x

Auburn

Inlet Station

CULPEPER COUNTY

EWELL
XXX

2

Culpeper Court House

LONGSTREET
XXX

1

Mount Pony

In late May and early June 1863, the Confederate Army of Northern Virginia began to move in secret from Fredericksburg to Culpeper County, 30 miles west. Its vanguard was Stuart's Cavalry Division, which camped in the vicinity of Brandy Station on the evening of June 8, 1863. Most of the cavalry of the Army of the Potomac, already in Fauquier County, just to the northeast of Culpeper County, moved toward Beverly and Kelly's fords on the Rappahannock River on June 8.

5 miles

5km

N

16

urging a negotiated end to the war. At the very least, the farmers of central and northern Virginia might gain time to plant, and even harvest, a crop without Yankee intruders. It would give the farmers of Maryland and Pennsylvania the opportunity to feed, involuntarily, Lee's famished men and to supply horses and mules for the cavalry, artillery and supply trains. The North indeed was a land of milk and honey compared to the devastated northern half of Virginia and the overburdened southern half. Seizing the strategic initiative, even winning a victory, in the East might relieve some of the pressure in Mississippi by forcing the Union high command to bring back some of Grant's men. One of Lee's staff officers succinctly sketched Lee's choice: "So, if General Lee remained inactive, both Vicksburg and Richmond would be imperiled, whereas if he were successful north of the Potomac, both would be saved."

Such a giant raid was a gamble of course. Lee would be operating in enemy territory with an extenuated supply line. A defeat there might prove calamitous. But Lee knew that time was running out for the Confederacy. She had few resources left of men, horses, railroads and industrial capacity. The Union naval blockade had closed most of her ports, depriving the South of both foreign exchange and scarce civilian and military goods. Hope of European intervention had evaporated. Lee and his closest generals worked out a plan of operations that would bring their army north of the Potomac with the least danger of being caught on the march by Union forces. First, it would be necessary secretly to move the army, some 80,000 in number, northwestward to Culpeper County. Then the army must cross the obstacle of the Rappahannock by its upper fords to avoid being caught upon the river in mid-passage. The next step would be to cross into the Shenandoah Valley via several gaps in the Blue Ridge Mountains. The Blue Ridge itself would mask the army's march down to the Potomac. Along the way, it might be possible to sweep up the Union garrisons in the Lower Shenandoah. Across the Potomac was the Maryland and Pennsylvania extension of the Shenandoah Valley, the rich Cumberland Valley. The Cumberland Valley led to the heartland of Pennsylvania.

The Confederate cavalry would play a key role in this great sweeping movement. It would hide the initial marches and then guard the right flank. It would hold, perhaps by itself, the Blue Ridge passes so that Union horsemen could not discern Lee's purpose in the Shenandoah. It would also keep an eye on Hooker's Army and its reactions to Lee's offensive. Once on Northern soil it would be the feelers, the scouts, as well as the initial foragers of the invasion. The five regular brigades of Stuart's division, supplemented by the irregulars of Jenkins and the "mounted infantry" of Imboden, both of whom would join Lee west of the Blue Ridge, would give Lee over 12,400 horsemen. Lee ordered the cavalry, the vanguard of the campaign, to cross the Rappahannock on June 9.

Major-General James Ewell Brown Stuart was a dashing and competent chief of cavalry in Lee's Army of Northern Virginia. Stuart's friend, General William Dorsey Pender, said of Brandy Station, "I suppose it is alright that Stuart should get all the blame, for when anything handsome is done he gets all the credit. A bad rule either way. He however retrieved the surprise by whipping them in the end." (Library of Congress)

OPPOSING COMMANDERS

Brigadier-General John Buford commanded the Right Wing of the Union force that attempted "to disperse and destroy" Stuart's cavalry in Culpeper, County, Virginia. His wing crossed the Rappahannock River at Beverly Ford. (Library of Congress)

UNION COMMANDERS

Lincoln appointed Major-General Joseph Hooker as commander of the Army of the Potomac at the end of January 1863 because of his demonstrated aggressiveness, his supreme self-confidence and perhaps because no one else wanted the burdens of the office. At Chancellorsville, at the start of May 1863, the hard-luck Army of the Potomac endured yet another defeat. Lee soundly thrashed "Fighting Joe" Hooker's splendid and much larger force. Contributing to the disaster was Hooker's paucity of cavalry: he had too few horsemen to scout and screen effectively. Hooker had dispatched his other cavalry on a raid deep behind Lee's army. Naturally Hooker looked for scapegoats after his defeat. He sacked the commander of the Cavalry Corps, George Stoneman, and replaced him with Brigadier-General Alfred Pleasonton. He then ordered Pleasonton to destroy the Confederate cavalry.

Pleasonton had been provisional commander of the Cavalry Corps of the Army of the Potomac for only two weeks at the time of the battle of Brandy Station To the job he brought much experience: fighting Mexicans, Indians, troublemakers in Kansas and Confederates. During the Peninsula Campaign, Major Pleasonton showed skill, dash and courage, and earned promotion to brigadier-general. Intensely ambitious, he cultivated a symbiotic relationship with some reporters. Consequently many newspaper readers came to think of him as a modern cavalier. But his talent for self-promotion often included lying to impress his superiors. He boasted that he alone, with a few batteries, had prevented Stonewall Jackson destroying the Union Army at Chancellorsville. Though many officers and men were outraged by this lie, Hooker believed him. Such deviousness did not escape the attention of many of his fellow officers. One colonel complained in a letter home that he "never had such a disgust in me before" after he heard that Pleasonton had been promoted to corps command. Another wrote to his mother that Pleasonton was " notorious as a bully and toady." What he lacked in integrity, he made up in sartorial splendor. He usually sported a natty straw hat, waxed mustaches, kid gloves and a riding whip. Seniority and his imaginative after-action reports had carried him to his present position. Oddly, he was almost invisible as commander during the battle of Brandy Station. In fact the Gettysburg campaign would offer numerous examples of Pleasonton's fitness, or unfitness, for such an important job as Cavalry Corps commander. Fortunately, able subordinates helped fill the gap at the battle of Brandy Station.

Pre-eminent among them was Brigadier-General John Buford. As capable as he was tough, Buford was a superb cavalryman, perhaps the best the Union had. He too was Regular Army, a comrade of Pleasonton in the prewar 2nd Dragoons. One admiring subordinate remembered, "It was always reassuring to see him in the saddle when there was any chance of a good fight." He was especially good at ferreting out enemy intelligence. On one raid he had captured "Jeb" Stuart's prized plumed hat, and almost its owner. Buford had fought well so far in the war. But greater rank had eluded him, partly from bad luck, partly because he had been born in the Southern, if Unionist, slave state of Kentucky. His fellow soldiers liked him. One of his comrades wrote of him that a single word of praise from him was "more valued to his officers than a brevet from the War Department." He would manage the right half of the Union troops at Brandy Station, with Pleasonton in tow.

Buford's temporary commander of the 1st Division was the proficient but crusty Colonel Benjamin Franklin "Grimes" Davis. He had been born and raised in the Deep South. His two brothers joined Mississippi infantry regiments at the outbreak of the war. Davis had wielded a saber most of his adult life and carried part of an Apache arrowhead in his body. He had won great fame by skillfully sneaking out of surrounded Harper's Ferry with several regiments of cavalry in September 1862. Along the way he used darkness and his thick Mississippi accent to capture a Confederate ordnance train of 97 wagons. Davis was reputed to be a martinet. But he possessed that most vital characteristic of a horse soldier: he liked to fight. Buford wrote after his death that he was "a thorough soldier, free from politics and intrigue … a bright star in his profession." During the battle he would command both the 1st Division and the 1st Brigade of that division.

Colonel Thomas Devin, a former house painter who led the 2nd Brigade, was quiet but dependable and brave. Catapulted from brigade command to temporary division command during the battle of Brandy Station, "Old Tom" rose to the occasion and performed well.

Major Charles Whiting's Reserve Brigade was attached to Buford's column. It consisted of all the regular regiments of cavalry in the army and one elite volunteer regiment. Although a West Pointer, Whiting had worked at various civilian jobs before rejoining the army six years before the Civil War.

Pleasonton despised the commander of his 2nd Division, Colonel Alfred Napoleon Duffie, simply because he was a foreigner. Duffie had served well in several European armies—if you did not count his desertion from the French one. His commission to become a brigadier-general was wending its way through the War Department bureaucracy. He had been the Union star of the battle of Kelly's Ford three months earlier. His men respected his abilities and were amused by his tenuous grasp of English. Nor did Pleasonton like the temporary commander of Duffie's 1st Brigade, Colonel Louis (or Luigi) di Cesnola. Di Cesnola was a veteran of the Sardinian Army and had also served with the British Army in the Crimea. John Irvin Gregg, the colonel in charge of the 2nd Brigade—and cousin of General Gregg—had entered the Pennsylvania militia after sterling service with the US regular infantry in the Mexican War.

No one was more solid in appearance than the leader of the 3rd Cavalry Division, Brigadier-General David McMurtrie Gregg. An Old Testament beard and mournful eyes made Gregg seem older and wiser than his 30 years. His calmness under fire was legendary. One superior later called him "a man of unusual modesty, but of far more unusual capacity." He had proved himself on many a field in a sturdy, professional way, earning the nickname "Old Reliable." Gregg was a West Pointer and a former Indian fighter. His service under McClellan in the Peninsula and Maryland campaigns had enhanced his reputation.

The commander of Gregg's 1st Brigade, Colonel Judson Kilpatrick, was combative to the point of recklessness. The bantam Kilpatrick had come to be known as "Kill-Cavalry." The nickname was double-edged. Kilpatrick was

ever willing to pitch into the enemy; he was also
suspected of using up his own men and horses
to advance his career. Some officers in the army
considered him as much a "newspaper humbug"
and as ambitious as Pleasonton. One staff officer
considered him "a frothy braggart without
brains." In addition to being a toady, Kilpatrick
was a bully. He certainly knew the value of good
press. He would often write the accounts of his
flashy exploits for accommodating journalists. Yet
beneath the glitter and venality was sometimes a
capable officer.

A British soldier of fortune, Sir Percy
Wyndham, commanded Gregg's 2nd Brigade. The
Italians had knighted him for helping Garibaldi.
Colonel Wyndham, though somewhat of a fop, and a liar about his
credentials, was an able warrior and an excellent disciplinarian. Of course,
the nativist Pleasonton despised him too.

Hooker insisted that Pleasonton include in his force two ad hoc infantry
brigades led by excellent brigadier-generals: David Russell and Adelbert
Ames. The regiments comprising these two temporary brigades were the
cream of the veteran Union infantry, hand picked from the various corps of
the Army of the Potomac.

CONFEDERATE COMMANDERS

Hooker's counterpart was General Robert E. Lee, a man at the height of his
ability and prestige at the beginning of the summer of 1863. Renowned for his
audacity and his habit of surprising his adversaries, Lee had ascended to
command of the Army of Northern Virginia only a year before. During that
period, he had become the embodiment of "The Cause" and was recognized
in the North and South as a brilliant soldier. He had forged a team of senior
generals—Longstreet, Jackson and cavalry leader Stuart—that had raised the
hopes of all Confederates. Yet now Stonewall Jackson was in his grave; and
Lee would have to depend even more on his old captains and the new ones in
command. Still, the most lethal weapon in Lee's army was its leadership.

The cavalry component of Lee's army was a division consisting of five
brigades and a battalion of horse artillery. Lee was confident that he had the
best possible cavalry leader in James Ewell Brown Stuart, known as "Jeb."
Lee recalled: "He was always cheerful, always ready for work, and always
reliable." Vain but skillful, light-hearted but deeply religious, he was more
than a bit of an exhibitionist. He was an incurable romantic who liked to
flirt with women and seemed to his many admirers to embody the ideals of
a modern-day knight. In his career as a soldier, Stuart had received only one
wound, from a Cheyenne he attacked with his saber in 1857; the Indian shot
him with a pistol. Stuart enjoyed making fools of his Yankee opponents.
Twice he had led his men completely around their army. Nevertheless he was
an excellent outpost officer, keeping Lee apprised of enemy activity while
shielding his own army. Horse artillery under his direction played a key role
at Sharpsburg (Northerners called the battle Antietam). At Chancellorsville,
he took over Jackson's infantry after Stonewall's wounding and performed
extremely well. Stuart's subordinates admired both his skill and boldness.

ABOVE LEFT
Brigadier-General Adelbert
Ames was an accomplished
infantry officer who had won
the Congressional Medal of
Honor at First Bull Run. He led
the ad hoc infantry brigade
with Buford's wing. (Library
of Congress)

ABOVE RIGHT
Brigadier-General David Russell
led the ad hoc infantry brigade
with Gregg's wing. He had
served in the US Army for
18 years. (Library of Congress)

Brigadier-General Wade
Hampton, possibly the richest
man in the South, dedicated
his life and fortune to the
Confederacy. Without a
professional military education,
he became a great Confederate
cavalry leader. (Museum of the
Confederacy, Richmond,
Virginia)

The coming battle and campaign, however, would expose both strengths and weaknesses in Lee's Beau Sabreur.

Stuart's senior subordinate was Brigadier-General Wade Hampton of South Carolina. One of the wealthiest planters in the South, he had opposed secession, Yet he stood by his state when war came. He helped to raise and equip a "legion" soon after the fall of Fort Sumter. The Hampton Legion, a battalion of infantry, two squadrons of cavalry and a battery of artillery, had functioned remarkably at First Manassas. That battle showed that this aristocrat, who had not been to West Point, was a natural soldier. The Legion was broken up at the end of 1861 and its commander, an excellent horseman, transferred to the cavalry. Hampton was 45 years old to Stuart's 30 at the start of the Gettysburg campaign. Hampton thought Stuart was not serious enough and did not pay enough deference to his own age and experience. But each recognized the great abilities of each other. Hampton, like Stuart, preferred to lead from the front, even if this meant engaging in close combat. The men of his brigade were from North Carolina, South Carolina, Georgia, Alabama and Mississippi.

The two other "permanent" brigades in Stuart's force were mostly composed of Virginia regiments and were led by Lees. Brigadier General W. H. F. Lee, known as "Rooney" Lee, was the second son of Robert E. Lee. General Fitzhugh Lee, called "Fitz" Lee, was the army commander's nephew. Nepotism was not a factor here as both were good soldiers, bred to the saddle, with demonstrated skills as cavalrymen. At the time of the battle "Fitz" Lee was suffering from rheumatoid arthritis and had handed the reins of command of his brigade to Colonel Thomas Munford. Munford, an excellent soldier, was patently general material. "Rooney" Lee was a shrewd tactician. He would give ample proof in the coming fight that he deserved his job.

That spring two other brigades were brought to Culpeper County to reinforce Stuart's cavalry. Stuart, who got along well with Hampton and the Lees, disliked his two additional commanders. Brigadier-General William E. "Grumble" Jones led the larger brigade, which was the largest cavalry brigade in the division. Stuart considered Jones a cranky, old (Jones was 43), slovenly and profane country bumpkin who fell down in disciplining his brigade and providing a good example for it. Jones thought Stuart too much a glory-hunting dandy. Jones' Brigade, which usually operated in the Shenandoah Valley of Virginia, had just returned from a long and successful raid into the mountains of Western Virginia. Its men welcomed the opportunity to rest up and to fatten their horses in the lush grazing-grounds of Culpeper County.

Stuart was more concerned about Brigadier-General Beverly Robertson. Robertson, a native Virginian, had been with the army the previous year, when he had shown Robert E. Lee and Stuart that he was sometimes able, sometimes incompetent. Transferred out, Robertson was back with a small brigade of two large and green North Carolina regiments sent to flesh out Lee's cavalry for the campaign.

Stuart's command was larger than it had ever been, and he was confident that his officers and men could handle anything the Union might push his way. Events would prove that he may have been overconfident.

Brigadier-General Beverly Robertson had served in Stuart's cavalry division in 1862. He rejoined Lee's Army at the start of the Gettysburg campaign. Stuart doubted his abilities as a cavalry commander. (Library of Congress)

OPPOSING FORCES

UNION FORCES

The United States Army had long had a tradition of using horsemen as dragoons: soldiers who rode to a fight and could dismount to use their firearms. In the conquest of the West, a few small regiments of dragoons (some of whom were named mounted rifles or cavalry), along with infantry and artillery in forts, were sufficient to protect settlers and travelers. Dragoons could punish effectively the Indian warriors of the prairies, mountains and deserts—if they could catch them. In the war with Mexico, 1846 to 1848, American regular dragoons fought brilliantly against the Mexicans, gaining glory with mounted charges. In 1861, the Federal Government renumbered the two regiments of dragoons, one of mounted rifles and two of cavalry sequentially and named them all "cavalry."

As with every war, the Federal authorities in 1861 thought the Civil War would be over quickly. A number of reasons were trotted out to justify not

This Union cavalryman "standing to horse" is not flashy, nor is his steed. But by the summer of 1863, he had become just as skilled as his Confederate counterpart. (Library of Congress)

Giesboro Point in the District of Columbia supplied the Army of the Potomac with all of its trained horses and mules by 1863. The largest depot of the Cavalry Bureau, it had facilities for 30,000 animals, including the ability to treat 2,650 sick beasts at a time. (Library of Congress)

raising large numbers of cavalry. Training cavalrymen was a time-consuming process; some volunteers even joined their regiments before they could ride horses. Many planners also doubted horsemen could be very useful in the woods, fields, towns and mountains of the country east of the Mississippi. Cavalry regiments, in addition, were expensive to raise and maintain. The government had no experience acquiring and maintaining large numbers of horses (and soon demonstrated minimal skill in those areas). Surely the Rebellion would be over before trained men and horses were ready. Hence it is unsurprising that the saga of the Union cavalry began slowly, and contained many blunders as well as defeats at the hands of their more agile and aggressive enemies.

One early and serious problem was a scarcity of good horses suitable for the cavalry. There were plenty of draft horses in the North, but pulling a plow, wagon or carriage does not produce the type of animal that cavalrymen need. Not until 1863 were the problems of supplying the cavalry with enough quality horses, weapons and equipment solved by the War Department creating a US Cavalry Bureau. It set up five huge remount depots close to the war zone, and sent educated and honest agents throughout the North to purchase animals. The depots also included veterinary facilities. Only after the horses and mules had been inspected and trained were they sent to cavalry regiments.

Civil War cavalry played a minor role in large battles. In no way were they like the thousands of heavy cavalry, chiefly cuirassiers and heavy dragoons seen on Napoleonic battlefields Even after the initial seasoning, many Union commanders continued to underestimate and misuse their cavalry. If anything, horsemen were overused. Cavalry made colorful escorts for generals and fine couriers. They could be utilized for reconnaissance, to escort baggage and supply trains, or to escort prisoners. Huge numbers were employed to picket and patrol the perimeters of armies, a complicated, exhausting and taxing chore. Often corps and division commanders, who controlled primarily infantry and artillery forces, had operational command of relatively small cavalry units. It is no wonder, then, that the cavalry should play a distant secondary role to the other arms. In the first two years of the war the Union cavalry were often bested by their Confederate opponents and suffered from poor morale. From 1863 onward, the horsemanship, professionalism and pugnacity of the horsemen in blue began to improve.

Not coincidentally, experts asserted that it took two years to make a cavalry regiment combat ready. Ironically, it was the author of the "dead cavalryman" crack, Major-General Joseph Hooker, who dramatically improved the Union cavalry in the East. One of his greatest accomplishments as an army leader in rebuilding his bruised and beaten army was to create for the first time a cavalry corps. Lee's army had long had a counterpart in the cavalry division of Stuart.

CONFEDERATE FORCES

The Confederate horsemen often displayed a professionalism in performing mundane duties and a panache that made the Yankees envious. While Confederate uniforms were often anything but uniform, their horses were usually in much better shape than those of the Northerners. Before the war, horse racing was popular in the South and produced horses bred for speed and stamina. Since the Southerners usually supplied their own horses, often from home (but sometimes captured from Union troops), they took better care of them. If the enemy killed a soldier's horse, the Confederate government would reimburse him for the value of the beast. But if the horse became permanently lame or died from sickness, the soldier had to pay for a replacement on his own. Thus a Confederate cavalryman was risking not only his life but also a very expensive piece of personal property by serving the cause. A soldier who lost his animal could go home on "horse leave" to procure another. He could be gone for weeks, even months if he had to journey home to the Deep South, and he might never return. The South, though a predominantly rural region, was running out of suitable animals by 1863. Stuart even set up an equine hospital south of Charlottesville, Virginia, in 1863 to slow the attrition of horses. Once dismounted, a cavalryman served in "Company Q" of his regiment until he received a recuperated horse, gained a captured Union horse or bought another. This company did various chores around camp and was usually the only company up to full strength in a regiment. Periodically, members of the company were sent to join the infantry or artillery—the final indignity for a horseman. Confederate cavalry units were thus chronically under strength. The desire to acquire horses from their foes shaped both tactical and even strategic plans. The Confederates started the war with an edge in both horsemanship and self-confidence. Aristocratic youngbloods gravitated toward the arm that would make them feel like cavaliers and brought excellent horses with them. Confederate cavalry soon acquired a reputation for daring if not discipline. Successful and famous raids like those of "Jeb" Stuart cemented the sense of superiority over the Yankees.

HOW CAVALRY WERE USED

At the beginning of the war, both the Union and Confederacy formed cavalry regiments of ten companies (the word troop was less common), each company had about 100 men. The Union soon changed to a 12-company organization, broken into three battalions of four companies each. Confusingly, the term battalion could also be used loosely to describe a group of several hundred men. Both sides formed squadrons of two companies, the company being more an administrative unit, the squadron a tactical unit. At Brandy Station no cavalry regiments were near their theoretical complement of over 1,000

officers and men. Half or less of formal strength was common. Many of the Union regiments at Brandy Station were short of a number of their companies. Some of those missing companies were on escort or some other detached duty. Others had been temporarily absorbed into other companies to compensate for the staggering attrition in horses during the Stoneman Raid.

Cavalry leaders of both sides quickly learned that new tactics were necessary for their mounted forces. The increased accuracy and range of rifled firearms and artillery had brought an end to battle cavalry as used by Frederick the Great, Napoleon and as recently as in the wars in the Crimea and Italy. Cavalry had learned to fight mounted and dismounted, in effect becoming dragoons. Usually they did not participate in battles, operating instead in front of and on the edges of armies. They could be scouts, raiders, escorts for wagon trains, and escorts for mounted generals. They were often adept at foraging and looting. They could, if necessary, block the enemy advance until friendly infantry arrived. But the glory years of the horse-soldier were nearly over; in less than 100 years, they would all be gone, replaced by aircraft, motorized and mechanized units.

The two basic mounted formations were column of fours and column of squadrons. The first, in which the ranks were four men across and about 100 men deep, was used on the march or while maneuvering, The second was the standard battle formation: two ranks deep, one squadron wide, all the other squadrons behind at intervals of about 30 yards. The standard "Hollywood" formation of all the men in a regiment in a two-deep line was rarely used because of the difficulty of moving through a countryside of woods, swamps, walls, creeks and farmsteads. In addition, it was difficult for the officers to control such a wide line. When a cavalry regiment dismounted—with some companies often kept mounted as a mobile reserve—one trooper out of every four held the reins of his own horse and three of his comrades. Cavalrymen were intensively drilled to change quickly from one formation to another.

This Union horse artillery battery is shown during the Peninsula Campaign in 1862. The picture reveals the great number of horses used by such a unit to pull the limbers, guns and caissons as well as to mount all the personnel. (Library of Congress)

This modern picture portrays a soldier of the Laurel Brigade, the nickname given in 1864 to the unit commanded by Jones at Brandy Station. Like his Union counterpart, he is ready for business. (*The Laurel Brigade*, courtesy of Keith Rocco)

Both sides at Brandy Station were armed in a similar manner. For mounted combat, cavalrymen carried light cavalry sabers and pistols. On foot, cavalry used carbines or pistols. Some Confederates carried more than one pistol, or a shotgun, or even a sawed-off musket. By 1863 Union cavalrymen primarily used six-shot Colt Army or Navy revolvers as pistols. Carbines were most often breech-loading Sharps or Burnside models. Confederates used what they could get: preferably what they could scrounge off the battlefield from the Yankees, then inferior Confederate-manufactured items or European imports. On outpost duty, troopers used carbines or rifles. In a skirmish with the enemy or in a melee, there was no intrinsic superiority of pistol over saber. Even a crack shot found hitting a moving mounted enemy difficult, and sabers did not need to be reloaded. Either weapon could be lethal. The saber had the advantage of intimidation during a charge; many defenders broke before a crowd of riders waving sabers reached them.

A typical cavalry charge against cavalry, a relatively rare occurrence, usually ended with one side or the other breaking and bolting before contact. A cavalry charge would start at a walk to maintain cohesion, gradually gain speed and reach the gallop only in the last 50 yards. If hand-to-hand combat ensued, the struggle could be confusing, vicious and protracted. If one side committed reserve squadrons or regiments to the fray, they often carried the day.

By 1863 the Confederacy had started to run out of horses, men and good quality firearms. At the same time Union equipment, morale and numbers were growing. In late 1863. the Yankees would begin to replace their single-shot breech-loading carbines with repeating carbines. The Spencer and Henry repeaters could pour out a hail of lead in a short time and sometimes give cavalry the ability to fight infantry. Repeaters, more than anything else, changed cavalry tactics during the war.

By 1863 cavalry on both sides had learned not to assault large units of infantry. Infantry rifled muskets greatly outranged carbines and pistols, and rifles were more accurate. If an infantry unit could be caught running, wavering, or on its flank or rear, mounted cavalry had a chance of success. Attacking deployed artillery also was tricky. Batteries could spew out a tremendous volume of shells and canister to their front, and needed to be charged from the flank.

Both sides at Brandy Station had batteries of horse artillery. Because the South had trouble supplying horses for artillery teams as well as horses to ride, Confederate horse artillery (and light artillery) batteries were standardized at four field pieces each, usually two less than their enemy counterparts. The guns were whatever calibers were available. By 1863, most Union horse artillery batteries consisted of six 3in. Ordnance Rifles, guns that were comparatively light and accurate. The most technically proficient and best drilled of the arms in the Union Army was the artillery. Confederate artillerists were hampered by mixed ammunition for different field pieces within a battery and poor fuses for shells. Confederate fuses had an alarming propensity to go off early or not at all.

ORDERS OF BATTLE AT BRANDY STATION UNION

CAVALRY CORPS, ARMY OF THE POTOMAC, BRIGADIER-GENERAL ALFRED PLEASONTON c.8,000 cavalry, 3,000 infantry attached, 34 guns, 700 gunners

Right Wing (troops crossing at Beverly Ford) Brigadier-General John Buford.
c.3,918 cavalry, 1,500 infantry, 16 guns (c.350 gunners)
1st Division, Colonel Benjamin F. "Grimes" Davis, acting commander, 2,061 men, six guns
    1st Brigade, Colonel Benjamin F. "Grimes" Davis
        8th Illinois Cavalry, Captain Alpheus Clark
        3rd Indiana Cavalry (six companies), Major William S. McClure
        8th New York Cavalry, Major Edmund M. Pope
        9th New York Cavalry (five companies), Major William B. Martin
        3rd (West) Virginia Cavalry (two companies), Captain Seymour B. Conger
        Vincent's Horse Artillery Battery (B & L Consolidated, 2nd US), Lieutenant Albert O. Vincent
    2nd Brigade, Colonel Thomas C. Devin
        6th New York Cavalry (four companies), Major William E. Beardsley
        17th Pennsylvania Cavalry (ten companies), Colonel Josiah H. Kellogg

Reserve Brigade, Cavalry Corps, Major Charles J. Whiting, acting commander, 1,857 men, four guns
    1st United States Cavalry (ten companies), Captain Richard S. Lord
    2nd United States Cavalry, Captain Wesley Merritt
    5th United States Cavalry (six companies), Captain James E. Harrison
    6th United States Cavalry, Captain George C. Cram
    6th Pennsylvania Cavalry, Major Robert Morris, Jr.
    Elder's Horse Artillery Battery (E, 4th US), Lieutenant Samuel S. Elder

Ad hoc brigade of Brigadier-General Adelbert Ames, c.1,500 men, six guns

    86th New York Infantry, Major Jacob H. Lansing

    124th New York Infantry, Lieutenant-Colonel Francis M. Cummins

    above two units commanded by Colonel Augustus Van Horne Ellis

    2nd Massachusetts Infantry, Major Charles R. Mudge

    3rd Wisconsin Infantry, Major Edwin L. Hubbard

    above two units commanded by Lieutenant-Colonel Martin Flood

    33rd Massachusetts Infantry, Colonel Adin B. Underwood

    Graham's Horse Artillery Battery (K, 1st US), Captain William M. Graham

Left Wing (troops crossing at Kelly's Ford) Brigadier-General David McM. Gregg c.4,063 cavalry, c.1,500 infantry, 18 guns (c.350 gunners)

2nd Division, Colonel Alfred N. Duffie, 1,893 men, six guns

    1st Brigade, Colonel Luigi P. di Cesnola

        1st Massachusetts Cavalry (eight companies), Lieutenant-Colonel Greely S. Curtis

        6th Ohio Cavalry(ten companies), Major William Steadman

        1st Rhode Island Cavalry, Lieutenant-Colonel John L. Thompson.

        4th New York Cavalry, Colonel Luigi P. di Cesnola—regiment not present

    2nd Brigade, Colonel John Irvin Gregg

        3rd Pennsylvania Cavalry, Lieutenant-Colonel Edward S. Jones

        4th Pennsylvania Cavalry, Lieutenant-Colonel William E. Doster

        16th Pennsylvania Cavalry (dismounted), Major William H. Fry

        Pennington's Horse Artillery (Battery M, 2nd US), Lieutenant Alexander C. Pennington

3rd Division, Brigadier-General David McM. Gregg, 2,170 men, six guns

    Martin's Battery (6th New York Independent), Captain Joseph W. Martin

    1st Brigade, Colonel H. Judson Kilpatrick

        10th New York Cavalry, Lieutenant-Colonel William Irvine

        2nd New York Cavalry, Colonel Henry E. Davies

        1st Maine Cavalry, Colonel Calvin S. Douty

        Independent Company, District of Columbia Volunteers, Captain William H. Orton

    2nd Brigade, Colonel Percy Wyndham

        1st New Jersey Cavalry, Lieutenant-Colonel Virgil Broderick

        1st Pennsylvania Cavalry (11 companies), Colonel John P. Taylor

        1st Maryland Cavalry (eight companies), Lieutenant-Colonel James M. Deems

        12th Illinois, Colonel Arno Voss—regiment not present

Ad hoc brigade of Brigadier-General David A. Russell, c.1,500 men, six guns

    56th Pennsylvania Infantry, Colonel J. William Hoffman

    7th Wisconsin Infantry + 2 cos. 2nd Wisconsin Infantry, Colonel William Robinson

    6th Maine Infantry, Colonel Hiram Burnham

    119th Pennsylvania Infantry, Colonel Major Henry P. Truefitt, Jr.

    5th New Hampshire & 81st Pennsylvania Infantry, Colonel Edward E. Cross

    Fuller's Horse Artillery Battery (C, 3rd US), Lieutenant William D. Fuller

In support, not under Pleasonton's command:

2nd Brigade, 1st Division, 5th Army Corps, Army of the Potomac, reinforced with the 1st Michigan Infantry Regiment, Colonel Jacob B. Sweitzer, c.2,000 men

CONFEDERATE

CAVALRY DIVISION, ARMY OF NORTHERN VIRGINIA, MAJOR-GENERAL JAMES E. B. STUART,

*c.*10,300 cavalry, 20 guns, 527 gunners

Jones' Brigade, Brigadier-General William E. "Grumble" Jones, *c.*1,730 men

    6th Virginia Cavalry, Major Cabell E. Flournoy

    7th Virginia Cavalry, Lieutenant-Colonel Thomas C. Marshall

    11th Virginia Cavalry, Colonel Lunsford L. Lomax

    12th Virginia Cavalry, Colonel Asher W. Harman

    35th Virginia Cavalry Battalion, Lieutenant-Colonel Elijah V. White

"Rooney" Lee's Brigade, Brigadier-General William H. F. "Rooney" Lee, 1,903 men

    2nd North Carolina Cavalry, Colonel Solomon Williams

    9th Virginia Cavalry, Colonel Richard L.T. Beale

    10th Virginia Cavalry, Colonel James Lucius Davis

    13th Virginia Cavalry, Colonel John R. Chambliss

    15th Virginia Cavalry, Major Charles R. Collins—not present

Hampton's Brigade, Brigadier-General Wade Hampton, 2,575 men

    Cobb's Legion Georgia Cavalry, Colonel Pierce M. B. Young

    1st North Carolina Cavalry, Colonel Laurence S. Baker

    1st South Carolina Cavalry, Colonel John L. Black

    2nd South Carolina Cavalry, Colonel Matthew C. Butler

    Jeff Davis Legion, Mississippi Cavalry, Lieutenant-Colonel Joseph F. Waring

    Phillip's Legion Georgia Cavalry, Colonel W. W. Rich—not present

Fitzhugh "Fitz" Lee's Brigade, Colonel Thomas T. Munford, 2,264 men

    1st Virginia Cavalry, Colonel James H. Drake

    2nd Virginia Cavalry, Lieutenant-Colonel James W. Watts

    3rd Virginia Cavalry, Colonel Thomas H. Owen

    4th Virginia Cavalry, Colonel Williams C. Wickham

    5th Virginia Cavalry, Colonel Thomas L. Rosser—not present

Robertson's Brigade, Brigadier General Beverly Robertson, *c.*1,308 men

    4th North Carolina Cavalry, Colonel Dennis C. Ferebee

    5th North Carolina Cavalry (11 companies), Colonel Peter G. Evans

Stuart Horse Artillery, Major Robert F. Beckham c.527 men, 20 guns

    Breathed's Virginia Battery (1st Stuart Horse Artillery), Captain James Breathed

    McGregor's Virginia Battery (2nd Stuart Horse Artillery), Captain William M. McGregor

    Chew's Virginia Battery (The Ashby Artillery), Captain Roger Preston Chew

    Moorman's Virginia Battery (The Lynchburg Artillery or Beauregard Rifles), Captain Marcellus Moorman

    Hart's South Carolina Battery (The Washington Artillery), Captain James F. Hart

THE BATTLE OF BRANDY STATION

BUFORD'S MORNING ATTACKS

At dawn on June 8, Captain Ulric Dahlgren of Hooker's staff hand delivered final permission for Pleasonton to launch his attack against the Confederate cavalry in Culpeper County. Pleasonton was waiting with General Buford, the divisions of Davis and Gregg and the Reserve Brigade near Warrenton Junction, about ten miles from the Rappahannock. He immediately ordered Buford to march to the river at Beverly Ford with Davis's 1st Division and the Reserve Brigade. The ad hoc brigade of infantry led by General Ames was to join this column halfway to the river. Pleasonton sent Gregg's Division to Kelly's Ford to meet Duffie's Division and the infantry of the Left Wing. Pleasonton established dawn on June 9 as the time for both wings to start across the river. Morale was high; Pleasonton sent word to Hooker that his men were eager to "pitch in."

After linking up with the infantry, Buford's column stealthily continued their approach march into the evening of the 8th. They camped within a mile of Beverly Ford late that night. The wooded bluffs between them and the river hid the 6,000 Union troops from anyone on the south bank of the Rappahannock. As far as Pleasonton could tell, the enemy cavalry near Culpeper Court House knew nothing of their presence. Along the way Buford's column had taken the usual security precaution of detaining numerous civilians and had left detachments to cover the rear. It had encountered no Confederate scouts. That night alongside the river was a cold bivouac. No fires were allowed, and the officers were instructed to keep the men quiet. One officer, Captain Daniel Oakey of the 2nd Massachusetts Infantry, did not prevent some of his men lighting a fire to boil coffee and was placed under arrest. Some of the soldiers munched hard tack and drank cold coffee. Most of the troopers slept about four hours with their reins tied to their wrists.

Surprises at the crossing

About 4am the men were woken without bugle calls. Word of the purpose of the expedition was passed around in whispers before the short march to the river began. Pleasonton first sent a 30-man company of the 2nd Massachusetts Infantry to creep to the ford to see if the way was clear and to locate the position of Confederate vedettes. They reported back that there were no obstructions nor signs that the Confederates knew the Yankees were coming. The way to Culpeper Court House seemed open.

Buford had picked Colonel Benjamin "Grimes" Davis, temporary commander of the 1st Division, to supervise the initial crossing and capture, kill or scatter the expected Confederate vedettes, and establish a foothold on the south bank so that the rest of the column would not be caught astride the river. Davis would force the crossing, if necessary, with a vanguard of two squadrons from the 6th New York Cavalry. It would be followed by Davis' own brigade, the Reserve Brigade of regular cavalry, Ames's infantry and, finally, Devin's small brigade. The horse artillery batteries would follow each of the brigades they were to support. Davis, commander of the 1st Division, thus was also the commander of the van of the Right Wing and commander of his own brigade.

The armies had used this ford before, and the officers knew what to expect. A lane led down from the bluff to the river, then made an abrupt right-angle turn south. The path proceeded for 50 yards between the river and an abandoned canal bed built several decades ago. It made another right-angle turn southward before entering the ford. The river here was only 25 yards wide, and even though the banks had been cut down to allow passage to the ford, they were still steep and the road narrow. The bottom of the ford had been lined with stones to improve the footing and prevent wagons (and artillery) from getting stuck in the river. The gurgling of water over a low dam not far upstream helped muffle the inevitable sounds coming from thousands of slowly moving men, animals and artillery. The men had tied down their saber scabbards and canteens to reduce noise, spoke only in whispers, walked lightly and carefully, and tried to control the whinnying of their horses. A heavy mist and the poor visibility at first light also helped

Borcke awakens Stuart on Fleetwood Hill. This print from Borcke's memoir of the events typically portrays the adjutant in a prominent role. (From *Die Grosse Reiterschlacht bei Brandy Station*, 1893)

Beverly Ford today is no longer a crossing of the Rappahannock River. We are looking at the Fauquier County side and the trace of where the bank had been dug out. (Photo courtesy Joseph W. McKinney)

them. Two Confederate horsemen on the south bank, however, heard enough to fire their pistols into the air and fall back to their nearby picket reserve. Because horses could not gallop in water three or four feet deep, the vanguard walked their horses across the ford. Once across, they surged up the embankment. The rest of the 4,000 Union troops quickly followed them. The Confederate picket reserve comprised about 30 men of the 6th Virginia Cavalry, from "Grumble" Jones' brigade. The rest of the brigade was camped two miles south of the ford along the Beverly Ford Road, near the Mary Gee House and St. James Church. The commander of the picket company, Captain Bruce Gibson, sent two couriers to warn his brigade. Gibson ordered the rest of his men to mount up and to draw their carbines and pistols. "Keep cool, men, and shoot to kill," he cautioned them. They were to inflict the first casualties that day, on mounted men of the 8th New York Cavalry who broke through the trees near the ford into open ground. Then Gibson and his men raced back south to their unit, their tripwire role accomplished. Davis dismounted some of the New Yorkers and ordered them to fan out as skirmishers. As the mist started to disperse, replaced in places by gun smoke, Davis ordered the rest of the 8th New York and the 8th Illinois Cavalry to head south on the Beverly Ford in column of fours at a rapid gait. A stream called Ruffin's Run, an old mill and thick vegetation near the ford precluded any other deployment.

Perhaps still glowing from the brilliance of his grand reviews, Stuart had already made two mistakes before he was jarred awake before sunrise by pistol, carbine and artillery fire near the ford. He had not stationed vedettes on the north bank of the Rappahannock at either Beverly or Kelly's fords. Far worse was the unorthodox location of the camp of the horse artillery battalion of his division. Apart from the few pickets at the ford itself, the battalion was the closest unit in the cavalry division to the enemy and it was camped only a mile and a half from the ford. But Stuart responded rapidly and efficiently to the sound of the gunfire to the north. Soon a courier arrived from General Jones, gasping out that Union troops had crossed Beverly Ford in force. Stuart ordered his camp dismantled and the headquarters' wagons to move with speed toward Culpeper Court House. He gave similar orders to the division wagon trains parked nearby. Three interrelated duties were paramount: find out what was happening down the Beverly Ford Road, assemble the scattered brigades of the division and find defensible ground until the situation was more lucid. He sent aides to the front for information. One of them, young Captain Will Farley, burst out, "Hurrah, we're going to have a fight." Jones already had his large brigade camped near the ford road. The artillery were sure to retire south on the same road. Couriers were sent to Hampton and "Rooney" Lee to hasten to the sound of the guns. Hampton's men were two miles south of Brandy Station. Lee had camped two miles north, many of his men near Wellford Ford on the Hazel River and near the Wellford House. As the 1st South Carolina Cavalry of Hampton's Brigade skirted Fleetwood Hill on its way toward the Gee House, Stuart redirected it toward Rappahannock Ford. Robertson's two-regiment brigade of green North Carolinians was two miles away, at the Botts place. Stuart ordered Robertson to watch Rappahannock Ford, Norman's Ford and especially Kelly's Ford. Several hours later, he sent word to Thomas Munford, whose brigade was seven miles away at Oakshade Church across the Hazel, to "come this way." A regiment of Munford's Brigade, the 4th Virginia Cavalry, had spent the night below Fleetwood Hill. Stuart directed it to join the 2nd South Carolina Cavalry and a throng of horseless cavalry of Hampton's Brigade in Brandy Station as a division reserve. After several hours Stuart rode to St. James Church to evaluate the situation firsthand. He left his assistant adjutant-general, Major Henry McClellan, on Fleetwood Hill with some couriers to relay dispatches.

Buying time on the Beverly Ford Road

Meanwhile Davis eventually placed his first two regiments in columns abreast on either side of the road, the 8th New York Cavalry on the right, the 8th Illinois Cavalry on the left, and ordered them forward through open ground

Heros von Borcke, late of the Prussian Army, was a valued assistant to Jeb Stuart. A very large man, it was said he rode the largest horse and carried the largest sword in the Confederacy. After he was gravely wounded at Middleburg, he left Stuart's service and eventually returned to Europe. (Library of Congress)

LEFT
Wade Hampton purchased four British Blakely 12-pdr guns to equip the artillery of the Hampton Legion, which later became the Washington Artillery of South Carolina. While accurate, the guns put great strain upon their carriages and frequently broke them. (Gettysburg National Military Park)

BUYING TIME ON THE BEVERLY FORD ROAD (pp. 36–37)

Most of Stuart's cavalry division was scheduled to cross at Beverly Ford early on June 9, 1863, to begin Lee's great move north. Sixteen guns of the Stuart Horse Artillery Battalion camped in an open wood about one-and-a-half miles from the Beverly Ford Road on the previous evening. Just why cavalry commander "Jeb" Stuart and their battalion commander, Robert Franklin Beckham, allowed them to bivouac in such an exposed position has never been explained. Four other pieces were separate from the main part of the battalion and split between the distant brigades of "Rooney" Lee and Thomas Munford.

Carbine fire from Union cavalry skirmishers rudely awakened the gunners and drivers at dawn on the 9th. The 400-odd artillerymen hurriedly pulled on their boots, grabbed a few personal belongings, and got their hundreds of horses, most of which are in a nearby pasture. The horses had to be hitched to the limbers, caissons and wagons before the battalion could escape. The battery commander of the Washington Artillery of South Carolina, Captain James Hart (**1**), reacted quickly. He ordered one of his four Blakely 12-pdr rifled field pieces into the road to buy time for the rest of the battalion to move off. Soon, battalion commander Beckham (**2**) ordered another of Hart's guns to join the first. As the guns fired canister at the Union cavalry about 300 yards away, help arrived. Around them on the shoulder of the road passed 150 men of the 6th Virginia Cavalry (**3**). About the same time, several hundred of the 7th Virginia Cavalry (**4**) broke through the trees to the west and hurdled towards the Union horsemen of "Grimes" Davis. Brigadier-General William E. "Grumble" Jones (**5**), brigade commander of both Confederate cavalry regiments, stopped briefly to reassure Hart and Beckham. Jones had also summoned the rest of his brigade to the point of crisis.

Canister from Hart's two guns as well as the attack of the two cavalry units halted the Union troops for a time. Beckham, retreated his battalion south up the Beverly Ford Road, then ordered Hart to withdraw his two guns alternately, firing as they retired. Courage and quick thinking saved the guns and alerted Stuart of his peril. If the Union forces had captured this Confederate artillery, Stuart's cavalry division would have been crippled at the very start of the Gettysburg campaign.

bordering the tree-lined road. Before long the New Yorkers spotted enemy troops ahead. Had they known the identity of the Confederates in the woods about 300 yards ahead, they might have rushed Stuart's horse artillery and captured the guns. Perhaps they feared walking into a trap in the half-light of dawn. Or perhaps they feared running into Confederate infantry or a line of waiting guns. In any case, they were cautious and merely peppered the tree line with carbine fire. Their caution, the quick reaction of artillery battalion commander Robert Franklin Beckham, the bravery of one of his battery commanders and the intervention of some Confederate cavalry saved the guns.

The horse artillerymen were awakened by bullets zipping over their heads and the shouts of Captain Gibson's band as it fled past them up the road. The 16 cannon and 400-odd gunners of the Stuart Horse Artillery had camped the night before in an open forest next to the road. Their horses, roughly 600 in number, were grazing in nearby pastures. The men frantically gathered them in, harnessed the teams to the limbers for the guns and caissons, saddled the rode horses, mounted up and beat a retreat south along the road. Captain James Hart of the Washington Artillery of South Carolina grabbed some of his men and wheeled one of his Blakely guns out onto the road. Soon the field piece was belching canister at the Yankees, forcing the 8th New York Cavalry to deploy into line and buying time for the rest of the artillery battalion. Major Beckham, who had succeeded gallant John Pelham, killed in the fight at Kelly's Ford in March, rose to the challenge of rescuing his men and guns. He immediately ordered another of Hart's guns to the road, and then turned to organize the hasty withdrawal. He ordered Hart to withdraw last his two pieces in alternate bounds, taking turns firing and retreating.

The 6th Virginia Cavalry also reacted quickly. The regiment had camped in the field west of the Gee House. Led by their commander, about 150 men of the regiment rushed toward the ford, some without boots, some without uniforms. They were soon joined by brigade commander Jones in a similar state of undress. Another Confederate regiment was heading in the same direction, thanks to a recent policy of Stuart's. He had ordered one regiment

Robert Franklin Beckham, a native of Culpeper County, had been in command of the Stuart Horse Artillery only three months at the time of Brandy Station. (Museum of the Confederacy, Richmond, Virginia)

After the war, veterans would often come together to reminisce. These veterans of Hart's Battery gathered in 1896. Undoubtedly they recalled their close call at Brandy Station. This picture includes the only extant image of ex-Captain James Hart, third standing man from the left, top row. (Photo courtesy of South Carolina Confederate Relic Room and Museum, Columbia, South Carolina)

Lieutenant R. O. Allen confronts "Grimes" Davis on the Beverly Ford Road. (*The Mortal Encounter*, courtesy of Don Stivers).

of each of his brigades to be saddled and ready to mount at first light each day. The "grand guard," as they were called, of Jones' Brigade that morning was the 7th Virginia Cavalry. They too moved forward quickly to the Beverly Ford Road. Both regiments galloped past Beckham's retiring battalion. "Grumble" Jones halted momentarily to tell Hart, "All right, Captain, we will take care of them, we'll give them hell." To the rear, the rest of Jones' Brigade—two regiments and a battalion—hurriedly prepared for battle.

Beckham withdrew his guns to a low open ridge 1,000 yards to the rear. On the east side of the Beverly Ford Road at this point sat the brick Gee House. To his front was 800 yards of gently rolling plateau in front of the woods: a perfect killing ground for artillery. Beckham positioned his four batteries on this ridge between the Gee House and a small but elegant, two-story, brick country church dedicated to St. James. He trained the guns on the Green's Mill Road, the Beverly Ford Road and the open ground. In the scramble from their bivouac, his battalion had lost a few horses, many tents, and a quantity of personal belongings. Notable among the latter was Beckham's field desk, which had tumbled out of a wagon onto the road. After Hart safely arrived at the ridge a few minutes later, Beckham discovered not a gun or gunner had been lost.

The men of the 6th Virginia Cavalry, followed by the 7th Virginia Cavalry, rammed into the 8th New York Cavalry on the Beverly Ford Road. The Confederates found the woods near the ford "swarming with the enemy's horsemen." A wild melee ensued. The 8th New York Cavalry, Davis's old unit and the largest regiment in Buford's wing, fell back toward the ford in disarray. But the Confederates found themselves flanked by other Union

troops and in turn broke contact. As the men of the 6th Virginia Cavalry retired up the road, one of them saw an opportunity. Lieutenant R. O. Allen noticed a Union officer at a bend in the road attempting to rally the 8th New York Cavalry. The Yankee faced back toward the ford and was isolated in advance of his men. Allen wheeled his wounded horse and dashed at the Union officer, who was "Grimes" Davis. When he reached Davis, the Union officer whirled in the saddle and slashed with his saber. Owen dodged the blow by swinging under his horse's neck, Indian style, and fired a pistol bullet into Davis's brain.

Among the changes at the battlefield, the church and the Gee House are gone. The trees and bushes in the middle distance that mark one of the courses of Hubbard's Run did not exist in 1863. Compare with the following picture drawn from the same perspective. (Photo by author)

The fatal wounding of Davis produced results far beyond the loss of one officer. Buford had to find Thomas Devin to take over command of the 1st Division and someone to take over Davis's Brigade. Devin had to designate a successor to command his own brigade. The Confederates seemed to be giving way; but the 1st Division was in turmoil, in no condition to pursue. Once the chain of command was reforged, the new Union commanders had to examine the ground ahead, deploy their division and brigades temporarily for defense, and re-form the troops disordered by the fighting. It now was obvious that Confederate cavalry and artillery were between Buford's Wing and Culpeper Court House. Pleasonton surmised that the Confederates had been told of his coming. He soon included this conjecture in a dispatch to Hooker that radiated anxiety and self-justification. Additional caution was needed; caution produced delay. Whiting's Reserve Brigade slowly made its way to the front. Most of Ames's infantry waded the river. Fourteen of Buford's 16 cannon crossed also. Buford sent a regiment of cavalry and a battery to hold a hill just west of the crossing. That hill plus the nearby Hazel River would anchor the right flank. Only then could Buford continue south on the Beverly Ford Road. In the nearly two hours since the wing had splashed across the Rappahannock, it had penetrated about a mile into Culpeper County. It was a warm morning; it would be a hot day. To the front

41

the 8th Illinois Cavalry fiercely counterattacked the two Virginia regiments. The Confederates rallied at the edge of the two-mile-wide woods that had held the camp of the horse artillery. Some Confederates dismounted and skirmished fiercely. Others seemed willing to contest Buford's progress toward Brandy Station with mounted combat. They held up Buford's men "with considerable sacrifice," Jones later reported. The roughly 2,000 men of Devin's Division supported by two batteries, nevertheless, put intense pressure on Jones's troopers. The 8th Illinois Cavalry finally drove most of the Confederates out of the woods. The 7th Virginia Cavalry fell back to the southwest while the 6th Virginia Cavalry retreated south up the road.

Salvos from Beckham's line of guns on the Gee House rise brought the Illinois regiment to a halt at the southern edge of the woods. Then the 12th Virginia Cavalry hit them. The fight among the trees didn't last long; the Illinois regiment made their enemy "git in a hurry." But the Yankees were brought up short by the last two units of Jones's Brigade, the 11th Virginia Cavalry and the 35th Virginia Cavalry Battalion. Other Union horsemen, the 3rd Indiana Cavalry and the 8th New York Cavalry, then joined the fracas in the woods and on the edge of the St. James plateau. Hundreds of sabers "gleamed and flashed in the morning sun" while hundreds of white puffs of smoke from firearms rose to the sky, one observer noted. The artillerymen on the Gee House ridge stood by their guns "in silent awe gazing on the struggling mass." Ultimately, the Confederate horsemen fell back and formed a line next to the guns on the Gee House ridge.

By now Buford had other troops to call on, and he hurried them into position. Two infantry regiments of Ames's Brigade tramped up the road from the ford. Buford placed them on the southern tree line: the 124th New York Infantry just west of the road, the 86th New York Infantry east of it. To their left he had already deployed the 1st Brigade of Devin's Division, minus the 8th Illinois Cavalry. He kept the tiny 2nd Brigade in reserve. He could find no good place to deploy artillery because of the trees. A section of Graham's Battery unlimbered near the road just outside the southern edge of the woods; it was driven off by fire from the massed Confederate guns.

These cavalrymen of Custer's Brigade are attacking a Confederate battery at Culpeper in the autumn of 1863. The melee between Beckham's guns and the 6th Pennsylvania Cavalry at Brandy Station undoubtedly looked like this fight. (Library of Congress)

About 7am, Buford called on Whiting's fresh brigade of regulars to clear the woods of Confederate stragglers. Whiting had only about two and a half regiments at hand. The 1st US Cavalry and part of the 6th Pennsylvania Cavalry were miles away in Fauquier County. The 5th US Cavalry was guarding the far right, near the Hazel River. Available were five companies of the 6th Pennsylvania Cavalry under Major Robert Morris, Jr.

Morris obeyed with alacrity the orders to attack the Confederate cavalry. Originally he was followed by the 6th and 2nd US cavalry regiments, but Pleasonton withdrew the latter unit for other duties at the last minute. The 365 men of the 6th Pennsylvania Cavalry successfully pushed the Confederates out of the forest, the 6th US Cavalry trailing behind. But something went very wrong after the Pennsylvania regiment came out into the big clearing on the other side of the trees. Their column of companies followed closely the retreating 35th Virginia Cavalry Battalion and the 11th and 12th Virginia cavalry regiments. The heat of battle, the dust and the hotheaded nature of their commander mixed to bring the regiment disaster. They continued their charge into the broad, grassy, natural amphitheater next to St. James Church. They and the following regiment, the 6th US Cavalry (only 276 strong), found themselves facing Beckham's deployed artillery, the cavalry brigade of Jones and also that of Hampton, who had placed his regiments in line east of the guns. Whiting's men were thus advancing into a mile-long concave angle of an enemy line of battle. The two Union regiments were enormously outnumbered. Yet they advanced, sabers drawn, with textbook discipline and uncommon valor. That they were not quickly swept

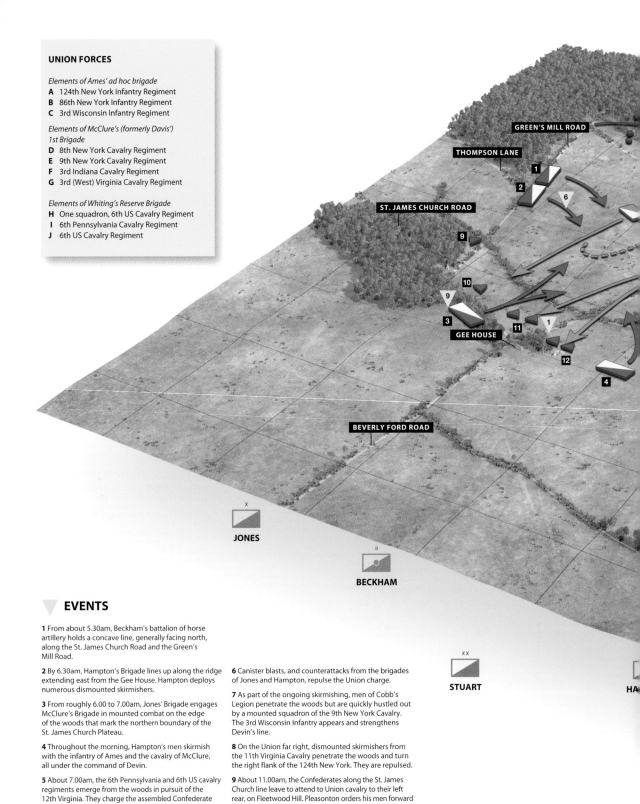

UNION FORCES

Elements of Ames' ad hoc brigade
A 124th New York Infantry Regiment
B 86th New York Infantry Regiment
C 3rd Wisconsin Infantry Regiment

Elements of McClure's (formerly Davis') 1st Brigade
D 8th New York Cavalry Regiment
E 9th New York Cavalry Regiment
F 3rd Indiana Cavalry Regiment
G 3rd (West) Virginia Cavalry Regiment

Elements of Whiting's Reserve Brigade
H One squadron, 6th US Cavalry Regiment
I 6th Pennsylvania Cavalry Regiment
J 6th US Cavalry Regiment

GREEN'S MILL ROAD

THOMPSON LANE

ST. JAMES CHURCH ROAD

GEE HOUSE

BEVERLY FORD ROAD

JONES

BECKHAM

STUART

HA

▼ **EVENTS**

1 From about 5.30am, Beckham's battalion of horse artillery holds a concave line, generally facing north, along the St. James Church Road and the Green's Mill Road.

2 By 6.30am, Hampton's Brigade lines up along the ridge extending east from the Gee House. Hampton deploys numerous dismounted skirmishers.

3 From roughly 6.00 to 7.00am, Jones' Brigade engages McClure's Brigade in mounted combat on the edge of the woods that mark the northern boundary of the St. James Church Plateau.

4 Throughout the morning, Hampton's men skirmish with the infantry of Ames and the cavalry of McClure, all under the command of Devin.

5 About 7.00am, the 6th Pennsylvania and 6th US cavalry regiments emerge from the woods in pursuit of the 12th Virginia. They charge the assembled Confederate cavalry and artillery on the Gee House ridge.

6 Canister blasts, and counterattacks from the brigades of Jones and Hampton, repulse the Union charge.

7 As part of the ongoing skirmishing, men of Cobb's Legion penetrate the woods but are quickly hustled out by a mounted squadron of the 9th New York Cavalry. The 3rd Wisconsin Infantry appears and strengthens Devin's line.

8 On the Union far right, dismounted skirmishers from the 11th Virginia Cavalry penetrate the woods and turn the right flank of the 124th New York. They are repulsed.

9 About 11.00am, the Confederates along the St. James Church line leave to attend to Union cavalry to their left rear, on Fleetwood Hill. Pleasonton orders his men forward to the former Confederate position but no farther.

ATTACK AND DEFENSE AT ST. JAMES CHURCH, JUNE 9, 1863
Devin's Division holds the line.

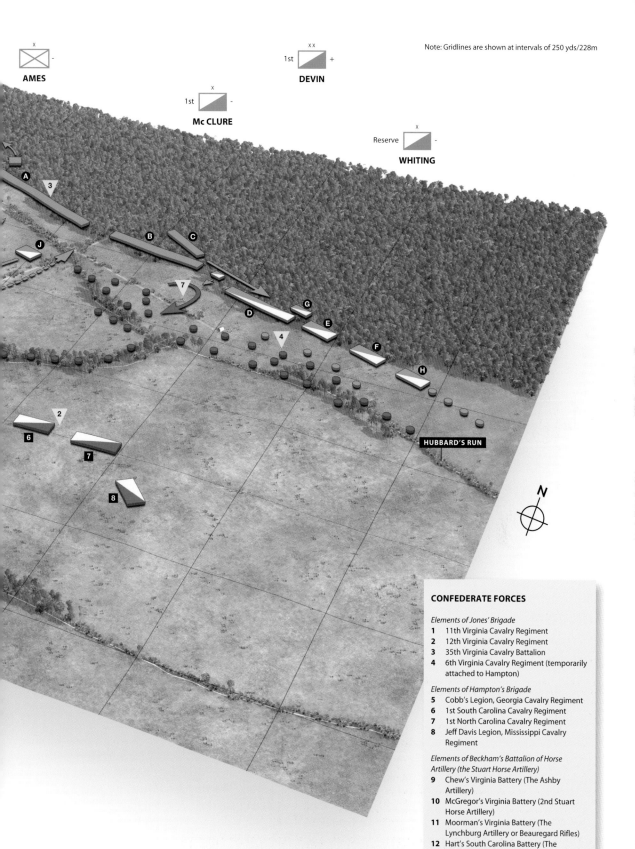

AMES

McCLURE

1st

DEVIN

1st +

Reserve
WHITING

Note: Gridlines are shown at intervals of 250 yds/228m

HUBBARD'S RUN

N

CONFEDERATE FORCES

Elements of Jones' Brigade
1   11th Virginia Cavalry Regiment
2   12th Virginia Cavalry Regiment
3   35th Virginia Cavalry Battalion
4   6th Virginia Cavalry Regiment (temporarily
    attached to Hampton)

Elements of Hampton's Brigade
5   Cobb's Legion, Georgia Cavalry Regiment
6   1st South Carolina Cavalry Regiment
7   1st North Carolina Cavalry Regiment
8   Jeff Davis Legion, Mississippi Cavalry
    Regiment

*Elements of Beckham's Battalion of Horse
Artillery (the Stuart Horse Artillery)*
9   Chew's Virginia Battery (The Ashby
    Artillery)
10 McGregor's Virginia Battery (2nd Stuart
    Horse Artillery)
11 Moorman's Virginia Battery (The
    Lynchburg Artillery or Beauregard Rifles)
12 Hart's South Carolina Battery (The
    Washington Artillery)

away by canister can be explained only by their front being partially masked by retreating Confederates. "Never rode troopers more gallantly," remembered Captain James Hart. One Union officer wrote that "Shells burst over us, under us and alongside … bullets were singing through the air like a hornet's nest." The charge may have been glorious, but it was hopeless. Major Morris was thrown to the ground and captured after his horse was hit by canister while crossing one of three small ditches in the field. Although some of the regulars got into Hart's Battery, they were driven out before they could cripple the unit. The 35th Virginia Cavalry Battalion hit the front of the two regiments while the 11th and 12th Virginia cavalry regiments roared in upon the Union right. One Confederate marveled that they fell back "as they came, with ranks well closed up." One Pennsylvanian had a different perspective. He called his return ride and close pursuit by Confederates a harrowing "race for life." The two battered Union regiments returned from "the handsomest charge of the day," as one man wrote, with jaded horses, uniforms ripped by tree branches, wounds and high losses. Apart from impressing soldiers on both sides, the charge accomplished little. It did give Devin's line a breather. It certainly convinced Buford that it would be difficult attacking out of the woods again. Undoubtedly both Pleasonton and Buford were wondering what had happened to Gregg and whether they themselves would have to fight Stuart alone.

If he could not break through Stuart's line at St. James Church, Buford was willing to try another tack. He would bring some of his men back north across Ruffin's Run, swing west and then south, and try to turn the left flank of the Confederates. He might force them back and get closer to Brandy Station, the assigned rendezvous with Gregg's column. He took Colonel Josiah Kellogg's small brigade (formerly Devin's), the Reserve Brigade, the large 8th Illinois Cavalry from what had been Davis's Brigade, and most of the artillery to the northern part of the Cunningham Farm. He could depend on Honest Tom Devin to hold stubbornly the line in the woods with roughly half the Right Wing.

Devin stands firm

Devin had deployed his men as best he could. His anchor was the two infantry regiments straddling the ford road. To their left was Davis's old brigade, now under Major William McClure. Most of his 1,000 or so cavalrymen were dismounted, taking cover behind the large trees of the forest and the brush at the edge of the woods. McClure left some of his troopers mounted, ready to plug any holes in his thin line as well as to launch a counterthrust. The 124th New York Infantry was in place west of the road. East of the road was the 86th New York Infantry, then the well-tried 8th New York Cavalry. Next to them was the 9th New York Cavalry, then the 3rd Indiana Cavalry; these last two regiments were at only half strength. Devin's left in theory stretched a mile to the bluffs above the Rappahannock but actually was "in the air." Two squadrons from the two New York regiments were deployed in a thin line of skirmishers over part of the distance along with a squadron of the 6th US Cavalry. The tiny 3rd (West) Virginia Cavalry, only one squadron strong, was in mounted reserve behind the 3rd Indiana Cavalry. The last regiment of McClure's brigade, the 8th Illinois Cavalry, was detached with Buford. There was no place along this line to deploy the Union artillery. Devin had two guns of Graham's Battery, but he was forced to keep them on the road, limbered and well out of sight of Beckham's lethal line of

metal. Another pair of guns, from Vincent's Battery, was in reserve to the rear. Soon after the repulse of the 6th Pennsylvania and 6th US cavalry the Confederates began to test the strength of Devin's position on both sides of the ford road.

War artist Waud portrayed the 1st Maine Cavalry skirmishing on foot with Sharps carbines at Middleburg, as much of the cavalry performed at Brandy Station. (Library of Congress)

Facing McClure's men from about 6.30am onward was Wade Hampton's formidable brigade. It also stretched eastward toward the river. Reduced to just three regiments when he first went into line of battle, Hampton soon regained the 1st South Carolina Cavalry, sent back by Robertson from the Kelly's Ford Road. He also had the use of the tired but reformed 6th Virginia Cavalry of Jones's Brigade. Hampton and Stuart confronted the tactical problem of facing an unknown number of Union troops across the Gee fields in the woods to the north. Never a practitioner of passive defense, Hampton sent out a tenth of his force as dismounted skirmishers to probe the enemy position. Then he increased the number of skirmishers. They soon found it necessary to hug the ground and take cover in dips in the ground to avoid the fire of the 86th New York Infantry. The rifled muskets of the Union infantry greatly outranged the Confederate carbines. Many skirmishers of the South Carolina regiment, on the other hand, were armed with Enfield rifles. They could match the range of the Union infantry and better the range of the Union cavalry. All the Confederate skirmishers, however, were in the open and confronting foes in the trees. The Union troops, though, were in a very thin line. The skirmishers from Cobb's Georgia Legion were aggressive enough to penetrate into the trees and there they met a sudden threat when a mounted squadron of the 9th New York Cavalry intervened, tried to ride them down and pursued them back into the field. The Union foray was brief, but the New Yorkers escorted some of the Georgians back to the trees as prisoners. The pressure on the Union cavalry was also lessened by the appearance from the rear of another of Ames's infantry regiments, the 3rd Wisconsin Infantry.

The white speck in the left distance is the shirt of a man standing just in front of the remains of the Cunningham-Green wall. Your perspective is that of Buford looking west on Cunningham Ridge. The interpretive signs, written by the author, were erected by the Civil War Preservation Trust. The trees 100 yards in front of the wall are modern growth. In the background is part of Yew Ridge and, beyond, the Blue Ridge Mountains. (photo by Peggy Beattie)

After Buford left the woods with half of his command, only the 124th New York Infantry, the "Orange Blossom Regiment"—so-called from their origin in Orange County, New York—was left manning a thin line on the edge of the woods to the west of the ford road. Though the soldiers were spread out as much as four feet apart, and hunkered behind large trees, shot and shell from Beckham's field pieces searched them out and caused casualties. A more direct threat then arose from a hoard of dismounted Confederate skirmishers of the 11th Virginia Cavalry. The men in gray and butternut advanced in open order toward the woods near the Green's Mill Road, on the right of the 124th. Then they suddenly disappeared from sight in a fold in the ground. The Union forces realized only too late what had happened when their enemy emerged to the right rear, thanks to a covered approach. The surprise attack, accompanied by the Rebel yell, compelled some Union infantrymen to make for the rear, but most of the Bluecoats were not so easily spooked. Their commander drew back two companies to face the west, in military parlance "refusing" his right flank. Confederate pressure increased until a rescue came from an unexpected source. Colonel Augustus Van Horne Ellis of the 124th commanded both his regiment and the adjacent 86th New York Infantry that day. He suddenly appeared with fresh troops on the left flank of the Confederates. Raising himself in his saddle, Ellis bellowed, "Give them the steel, my honeys, the brigade will support you." Ellis was bluffing. His fresh "brigade" comprised one company of the 86th. Resolute fire from the companies at the far right of Devin's defense, and perhaps Ellis's "orders," drove back the Confederates to their original position. Other Union troops, the newly arrived 2nd Massachusetts Infantry, entered the woods to link up with Ellis's men.

By mid-morning Stuart had tested Devin's line but had not tried to break it with an all-out attack. Devin had as many men as he was going to get: McClure's cavalry brigade on the left, Ames's infantry in the center and right. Two thousand veteran Union troops led by veteran officers held firm, though they expected a major assault. About 11am, the Union troops saw a startling sight. First, the Confederate skirmishers all along the line in front retired. Then most of Jones's Brigade hastily left to ride south, followed by most of the horse artillery. Not much later, Hampton's regiments left their place in the line east of the road. Trees screened the Union view of Fleetwood Hill, the Confederate destination a mile away. This new development could mean only that Stuart was reacting to a threat to his rear. That threat must be the arrival of Gregg's divisions and a tumult of cannon and small-arms fire in the direction of Brandy Station confirmed that fact. Pleasonton launched a careful advance south. He set up his new headquarters in the Gee House but did not move his troops much beyond St. James Church. This part of the Right Wing was not to intervene in either of the ongoing struggles for Fleetwood Hill: Gregg's attempt to seize the southern end of the ridge or Buford's effort to capture the northern end. For the troops under Devin and Ames the battle was all but over.

Buford swings west

After Buford crossed Ruffin's Run with a sizable portion of the Right Wing, he found two obstacles to his plan to turn the Confederate left: one was constrictive terrain, the other was yet another large brigade of Southern horsemen. Buford rode up to the top of a prominent open knoll that was the southern projection of a long, mostly treeless ridge that ran north–south on the Cunningham property. Grassy slopes ran down to boggy ground and to woods; a line of higher grassy knolls lay to the west, while the distant Blue Ridge Mountains overlooked the scene. The land was owned in absentia by Richard Cunningham and the ruins of his house, "Elkwood," burned the previous year by Union troops, lay along the ridge. The house of Cunningham's overseer, John Wiltshire, stood along Ruffin's Run near a stone wall. Buford did not like what he saw or heard from his officers on the knoll.

Several hours before, elements of the Reserve Brigade—the 2nd and 5th US cavalry regiments—had taken position behind the low stone wall that separated the Cunningham and Green farms. This north–south wall was only 500 yards west of Buford's knoll and just a mile from Beverly Ford. It ran between Ruffin's Run and low ground near the Hazel River, which was uncrossable here. The Union cavalry lining the wall suddenly found their relatively pleasant rear-echelon duty of guarding the rear of Pleasonton's force change dramatically after a mass of Confederate dismounted skirmishers (then termed "sharpshooters") appeared to the west and tried to capture the wall and Beverly Ford. The Union troops kneeling behind the wall found it a handy defense until the Confederates increased in number. The Union troops also began to run low on ammunition. Buford replaced the 5th by the battle-worn 6th Pennsylvania Cavalry, recently replenished by additional squadrons from across the river. "It was decidedly the hottest place I was ever in," said the commander of the 6th, who had barely escaped unharmed from the charge at St. James Church earlier that morning. But the Pennsylvanians did not hold on long. They and the 2nd US Cavalry were compelled to run for their horses and fall back across the fields to Cunningham Ridge. The stone wall was now a defensive position manned by the dismounted men of the 10th and 13th Virginia cavalry regiments.

"Rooney" Lee commanded the Confederate brigade. Courageous and resourceful, he possessed a zeal for combat and, from the Confederate viewpoint, he was the right man at the right place at the right time. The night before, two of his regiments had bedded down around the Wellford House and nearby Wellford's Ford on the Hazel River. The other two camped further west. He had acted fast after he received Stuart's alert that morning. Riding towards Beverly Ford, two miles east, Lee and his two regiments

Captain Wesley Merritt of the 2nd US Cavalry received a brusque answer when he summoned a Confederate colonel to surrender. In the background is "Farley," the Wellford House. (*Duel on Yew Ridge* courtesy of Don Stivers.)

descended Yew Ridge, crossed Dr. Daniel Green's farm and arrived before the Green/Cunningham wall at roughly 6.30 or 7am. The Confederates could plainly see the Union artillery on top of Cunningham Ridge, some of which temporarily forced back one of Lee's approaching regimental columns. After forcing the Union troopers to retreat, all four of Lee's units, the 9th, 10th and 13th Virginia cavalry regiments, and the 2nd North Carolina Cavalry, lined the wall with sizable mounted reserves of each regiment to the rear. Lee's small artillery contingent, a section of 12-pdr Napoleon guns from Breathed's Maryland Battery, unlimbered in a fold in the ground on Yew Ridge.

Soon after Buford arrived on the knoll, about 8am, he concluded, as he later reported, "the enemy threatened to overwhelm me." But he quickly collected, on and behind Cunningham Ridge, over two dozen squadrons of cavalry, ten pieces of rifled artillery and two companies of infantry—in all more than 2,000 men. He probably supposed that this was more than enough to guard the crossing, enough in fact to push the new Confederates out of the way. He could not know that "Rooney" Lee had 2,000 veteran horsemen of his own brigade, the 7th Virginia Cavalry (loaned by Jones) and two field

Buford attempts to link up with Gregg

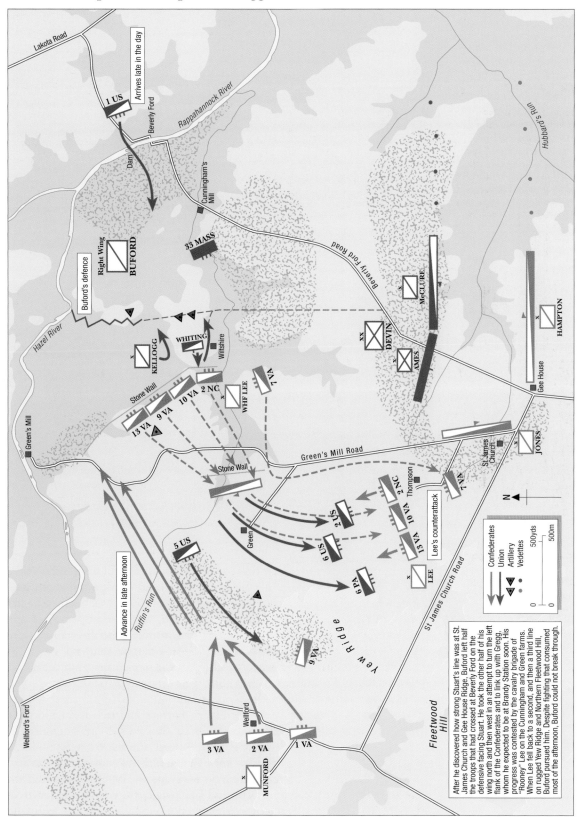

Lakota Road

1 US — Arrives late in the day

Beverly Ford

Rappahannock River

Dam Run

Cunningham's Mill

33 MASS

Right Wing — BUFORD — Buford's defence

Beverly Ford Road

x — McCLURE

Hubbard's Run

x — HAMPTON

Hazel River

xx — DEVIN

x — AMES

WHITING

KELLOGG

Wiltshire

Gee House

x — JONES

Stone Wall

2 NC

10 VA

WHF LEE

7 VA

9 VA

13 VA

Green's Mill

Green's Mill Road

Stone Wall

St. James Church

Thompson

2 NC

10 VA

7 VA

Advance in late afternoon

Green

2 US

13 VA — Lee's counterattack

5 US

6 US

x — LEE

Ruffin's Run

6 PA

Yew Ridge

9 VA

Fleetwood Hill

St James Church Road

3 VA

Wellford

2 VA

1 VA

Wellford's Ford

x — MUNFORD

Legend:
Confederates
Union
Artillery
Vedettes

N

500yds
500m

0 — 0

After he discovered how strong Stuart's line was at St. James Church and Gee House Ridge, Buford left half the troops that had crossed at Beverly Ford on the defensive facing Stuart. He took the other half of his wing north and then west in an attempt to turn the left flank of the Confederates and to link up with Gregg, whom he expected to be at Brandy Station soon. His progress was contested by the cavalry brigade of "Rooney" Lee on the Cunningham and Green farms. When Lee fell back to a second, and then a third line on rugged Yew Ridge and Northern Fleetwood Hill, Buford pursued him. Despite fighting that consumed most of the afternoon, Buford could not break through.

guns. Buford also learned that the rugged terrain in front of him: stone walls, Yew Ridge and northern Fleetwood Hill, would substantially aid any Confederate defense. While the half-mile long stone wall was manned by the enemy, its northern half was protected by marshy terrain that prevented any attempt to outflank the position. As a result any attacks on the wall must be channelled into the few hundred yards directly in front of Buford.

The Union general attempted to suppress the intermittent but annoying indirect artillery fire from Lee's two guns. This task was difficult because only the smoke from the fire of the Confederate guns indicated their hidden position. Even so, the four guns of Elder's Battery and two from Vincent's shelled the area of the smoke and partially suppressed the Confederate fire.

In his first attempt to regain the wall, Buford ordered fresh dismounted cavalry, this time from the 6th New York Cavalry, 17th Pennsylvania Cavalry and the rested 8th Illinois Cavalry, to dislodge the Southerners. A lack of cover defeated this attempt. The 2nd US Cavalry then tried and failed. It was almost 10am and Buford was stalled on Cunningham Ridge while the

The Wellford House was the headquarters of Major-General John Sedgwick (shown third from the right), the 6th Corps commander and Meade's senior subordinate, during the winter camp of 1863/64. (Library of Congress)

Confederates to the south increased the pressure on Devin, he decided to use infantry to break the enemy position. He summoned the 33rd Massachusetts Infantry and the remaining section of Graham's Battery, which had been guarding the eastern side of the ford. He placed the infantry unit astraddle Ruffin's Run, adjacent to his knoll. Three companies of infantry from Ames's Brigade had already been detailed to support the artillery and were lolling on the grass behind the guns. Buford called forward the two officers commanding them to his clump of staff on the knoll. Captain George Stevenson of the 3rd Wisconsin Infantry was the senior infantry officer. He was accompanied by Captain Daniel Oakey of the 2nd Massachusetts Infantry, earlier arrested for allowing his men to build a fire. Pointing to the wall, Buford enquired, "Do you see those people down there? They've got to be driven out. Do you think you can do it?" The officers scanned the wall and pointed out that the Confederates probably outnumbered their own hundred men by two to one. "Mind, I don't order you; but if you think you can do it, go in," replied Buford and they agreed to try. Stevenson had his men squirm on their bellies through tall brush along Ruffin's Run and a wheat field adjacent to the Wiltshire House. They were preceded by a handpicked group of ten of the best shots. When the sharpshooters got to the end of the wall, they suddenly popped up and threw a volley into the 2nd North Carolina Cavalry behind the wall. The rest of the Union troops ran forward with a cheer and those surprised Confederates who were not killed or captured darted back to their held horses. Buford had his wall.

Probably because he had seen the 33rd Massachusetts Infantry lining up across the creek, Lee had earlier pulled most of his men back to a new line, fronting the wall but several hundred yards to the rear, on Yew Ridge. As Buford's men regained the wall, the Union troops beheld an unexpected sight. Lee's second Confederate line, except for a small rearguard, formed columns

BUFORD ON CUNNINGHAM'S RIDGE (pp. 54–55)

By 7.30 am the Confederate defense of the area around St. James Church had stopped further progress by the Right Wing of the invading Union cavalry force. General John Buford realized that he was outnumbered, and breaking through the line of Confederate cavalry and artillery was problematical. Pleasonton's plan to link up at Brandy Station with the Left Wing, which had supposedly crossed at Kelly's Ford that morning, by the Beverly Ford Road would have to be revised. Buford took half of his men to his right in order to outflank the defenses near St. James Church.

The right of his line had been anchored along a low stone wall that separated the Cunningham and Green farms and stretched between Ruffin's Run and the Hazel River. The wall was only 1,000 yards from Beverly Ford. Dismounted Confederate cavalry of "Rooney" Lee's brigade, however, wrested it from Union control early in the day. The Yankee right flank then fell back eastward about 500 yards to a prominent ridge that paralleled the wall. It seemed likely that this ridge on the Cunningham farm eventually would be attacked by the Confederates. it was the final Union line. But Union reinforcements, rushed there by Buford and Pleasonton, soon formed a strong defense.

Buford dismounted on the knoll that crowned Cunningham's Ridge about 8am and surveyed the situation. Regaining the wall, he realized, was an essential step to turning the Confederate left at St. James Church and thrusting towards Brandy Station. Though he had plenty of cavalry and artillery, determined Rebel defenders defeated several attacks. Neither mounted or dismounted Union cavalry assaults nor the fire of several Union batteries could budge the enemy behind the stone wall. Then Buford summoned two nearby infantry officers and asked them whether their three companies could succeed where the cavalry had failed.

Many of the men on Cunningham Ridge know that Buford's calm demeanor and ever-present pipe disguise a bold and aggressive leader. Buford wears his famous "hunting shirt" (**1**) and points at the wall with his simple pipe. He is surrounded by members of his staff and that of corps commander Pleasonton. Adjacent to the bugler (**2**) on the right stands General Alfred Pleasonton (**3**). One of Pleasonton's aides, Lieutenant George Custer (**4**), wearing his characteristic red scarf, looks on with keen interest. The rifled field piece is part of Elder's Battery (**5**).

and headed for the rear. This happened as Devin saw the Confederates melt away to his front, and for the same reason; Gregg was at Brandy Station. Lee formed a third line closer to Fleetwood Hill.

Over the next four hours Buford slowly pushed back the Confederates. They resisted first on Yew Ridge, a series of high knolls west of the stone wall. They then stubbornly fought on the northern end of Fleetwood Hill. Buford led the men of the Reserve Cavalry Brigade, accompanied by Elder's Battery and part of Vincent's Battery and the Confederates grudgingly gave ground to the south. Most of the fighting was on horseback. But some was on foot in thickets and over yet another stone wall. Buford later claimed that he reached the crest of Fleetwood Hill and saw Brandy Station in the distance, about two miles away. In mid-afternoon Lee launched a powerful counterattack up from the fields of the Thompson Farm against the Union troops on northern Fleetwood Hill. The Yankees were forced to give ground after a prolonged mounted melee. "Rooney" Lee, leading from the front, received a pistol wound in the thigh, his immediate successor was soon shot out of the saddle and Colonel John Chambliss, Jr., of the 13th Virginia Cavalry, took over and fought just as boldly as Lee had.

By mid-afternoon, the men and, perhaps even more so, the horses of both sides were exhausted from pounding up and down the slopes on such a warm day. Each side had given as good as they had received. But Buford had neither outflanked the Confederates nor reached Brandy Station. Late in the afternoon, Pleasonton sent orders for Buford and his men to fall back to Beverly Ford. Soon after Buford began to retire, the three fresh regiments of Munford's Virginia brigade at last arrived near the Wellford House. Munford at Oak Shade Church had received Stuart's order to "come here" only at 10.15am and was never able to explain why it then took him nearly six hours to reach a battlefield five miles away. Had he arrived even a hour earlier, he might have cut off Buford's retreat and destroyed the Union troops on northern Fleetwood Hill. His performance was not striking even after arriving at the scene of action. After it reached the battlefield, Munford's Brigade collided with Lee's 9th Virginia Cavalry. After matters were sorted out, Munford gingerly followed Buford toward the ford but was brought up short by a large force of all arms at Cunningham Ridge. A fresh unit was also there; the 1st US Cavalry had recently crossed the ford. As the fighting sputtered out at this end of the battlefield, General Beverly Robertson arrived with one of his regiments. Sent by Stuart, he assumed command of the northernmost two brigades, though he had little to do. As the Union forces fell back, Buford rode up to Pleasonton. The corps commander informed his wing commander why he had decided to end the fighting. He also revealed what had transpired that long day with Gregg and the Left Wing.

Despite his youthful appearance, General Wesley Merritt was one of the most gifted cavalry leaders of the war. He was promoted from captain to brigadier-general three weeks after Brandy Station. (Library of Congress)

GREGG'S ADVANCE

The Pleasonton–Hooker plan for the Left Wing began to unravel even before the first Union soldier crossed Kelly's Ford. There would be plenty of blame later to be shared between David Gregg, commander both of the wing as well as the 3rd Cavalry Division, and his chief subordinate, Alfred Duffie, commander of the 2nd Cavalry Division. Only the commander of the infantry component of the wing, General David Russell, did not come out badly. But it's hard to find anything in his performance that stands out as a significant contribution toward victory that day. Yet the plan for the crossing of the

Routes taken by the cavalry divisions of Duffie and Gregg during the battle

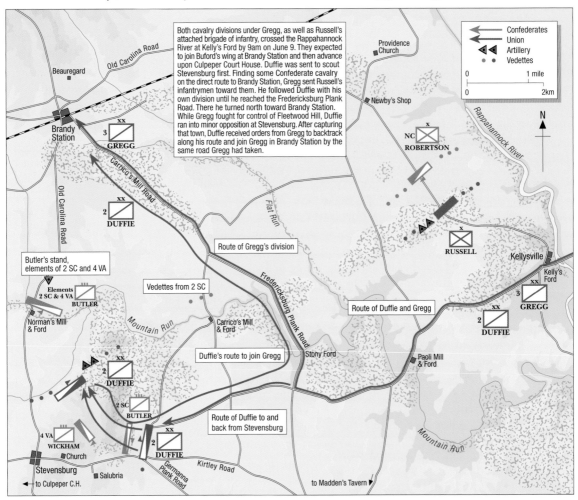

Both cavalry divisions under Gregg, as well as Russell's attached brigade of infantry, crossed the Rappahannock River at Kelly's Ford by 9am on June 9. They expected to join Buford's wing at Brandy Station and then advance upon Culpeper Court House. Duffie was sent to scout Stevensburg first. Finding some Confederate cavalry on the direct route to Brandy Station, Gregg sent Russell's infantrymen toward them. He followed Duffie with his own division until he reached the Fredericksburg Plank Road. There he turned north toward Brandy Station. While Gregg fought for control of Fleetwood Hill, Duffie ran into minor opposition at Stevensburg. After capturing that town, Duffie received orders from Gregg to backtrack along his route and join Gregg in Brandy Station by the same road Gregg had taken.

Confederates / Union / Artillery / Vedettes

0   1 mile
0   2km

N

Providence Church

Newby's Shop

Rappahannock River

NC ROBERTSON

RUSSELL

Kellysville

Kelly's Ford

Beauregard

Old Carolina Road

Brandy Station

3 GREGG

Carrico's Mill Road

Old Carolina Road

2 DUFFIE

Flat Run

Route of Gregg's division

Butler's stand, elements of 2 SC and 4 VA

Vedettes from 2 SC

Elements 2 SC & 4 VA BUTLER

Norman's Mill & Ford

Mountain Run

Carrico's Mill & Ford

Fredericksburg Plank Road

Route of Duffie and Gregg

3 GREGG

2 DUFFIE

Duffie's route to join Gregg

Stony Ford

Paoli Mill & Ford

2 DUFFIE

2 SC BUTLER

4 VA WICKHAM

Church

Stevensburg

Salubria

to Culpeper C.H.

2 DUFFIE

Germanna Plank Road

Kirtley Road

Route of Duffie to and back from Stevensburg

Mountain Run

to Madden's Tavern

Rappahannock was well thought out and clear on paper. The wing was to cross at first light and march the seven miles to Brandy Station to join Buford's Right Wing. Recalling the delay in seizing a foothold across the river during the Kelly's Ford strike in March, Hooker ordered a new technique. He told his engineers to loan the Left Wing two collapsible, canvas pontoon boats to ferry a few picked infantry across before the cavalry approached the ford. It was hoped these 30 men would cross without resistance and easily disperse the few Confederate vedettes on the south bank. This scheme worked perfectly. By dawn the Union troops were in full control of the ford.

Hooker had told Pleasonton to order Gregg to send at least a regiment ten miles west to the town of Stevensburg. This detachment would check out the likely roads that might bring Confederate infantry to Culpeper County. That reconnaissance accomplished, the detachment would rejoin the rest of the Cavalry Corps in its advance on Culpeper Court House. Gregg may have thought he was improving on Pleasonton's strategy—and amply protecting his own left—by increasing the strength of the Stevensburg probe to Duffie's full division plus a battery. He would send Russell's 1,500 infantry to Brandy Station by the direct road near the river. At the same time he would take his own division west, hit the little-used Fredericksburg Plank Road after crossing

Mountain Run and march north to Brandy Station. For further security, Hooker ordered an infantry brigade from 5th Corps to follow Duffie and Gregg to the Fredericksburg Plank Road and leave guards at key spots along the route. Gregg expected little Confederate opposition and may have split his force to avoid congestion on a single road to Brandy Station. It would make sense for Duffie to use the ford first before marching west to Stevensburg, and then have Russell cross and tramp northwest to Brandy Station, accompanied by a battery and a company of cavalry. Gregg would cross next and commence his march. Finally, General Sweitzer would bring up the rear with his brigade from 5th Corps. One of Duffie's regiments, the horseless 16th Pennsylvania Cavalry, would be left near Kelly's Ford to guard the wagon trains and pack mules of the two divisions.

For several hours, Gregg awaited Duffie's command. Pleasonton had told Duffie to make haste, use stealth on his approach march and also bring along his divisional wagons and ambulances: a recipe for confusion and delay. The

Colonel Matthew Calbraith Butler lost a foot at Stevensburg but stalled Duffie's Division just long enough. (Photo courtesy US Army Heritage and Education Center, MOLLUS Collection, Mass. Commandery)

troopers under Duffie were weary as they had marched the previous two nights and afternoon to avoid observation by Confederate sympathizers along the route. Most of Duffie's men slumped to the ground on the night of June 8 near midnight, still short of their goal. They again took up the march at 2am on the 9th. Fortunately, Kelly's Ford lay only five miles away in a straight line, and Duffie had taken a brigade over the same route in March. This time it took him until 5.30am to reach Gregg and Russell at the ford after a ten-mile march. To add further delay, Gregg had the other units of the Left Wing wait for Duffie instead of sending some across the river early. By the time Gregg got everybody across the Rappahannock, it was 9am and he was already more than three hours behind schedule. From upriver came the rumble of artillery fire the whole time, a clear indication that Buford had met serious opposition. Brandy Station was only about seven miles by road, even shorter across country. Furthermore, the land between Kelly's Ford and Brandy was mostly flat and open: excellent cavalry ground. But Gregg was unwilling to march by road directly to the sound of the guns with the whole wing, or to go across country to Brandy Station, or even reduce the size of the force destined for Stevensburg. He adhered to his original plan.

Duffie's groggy troopers and battery methodically plodded west on the Stevensburg Road. They waded across Mountain Run (Buford had once called it "a vicious little stream") at Paoli Mill, passed the turnoffs to Brandy Station via the Plank Road and Carrico's Mill Road and proceeded toward Stevensburg. They saw no Confederates, but Duffie began to feel the urgency of the situation. He told the officer in charge of his lead regiment, the 6th Ohio Cavalry, to send forward two squadrons to Stevensburg to see if there was any opposition there. Major Benjamin C. Stanhope led that vanguard of Union horsemen. He turned west after reaching the Germanna Plank Road (here called Kirtley Road), the main thoroughfare between Fredericksburg and Culpeper Court House. After crossing the prominent Hansbrough Ridge on the road, Stanhope halted his battalion on the lawn of a country church,

Russell's infantry brigade included these veterans of the 6th Maine Volunteer Infantry. (Library of Congress)

on a knoll that offered a panoramic view of the surrounding countryside. Five miles away to the north was the long ridge of Fleetwood Hill near Brandy Station. Directly to the west down the road toward the courthouse was lofty Mount Pony. Right beneath his gaze, slumbering peacefully, was the village of Stevensburg. No Confederates were in sight. Stanhope ventured into the quiet village. Instead of searching for Confederates west toward Culpeper Court House, on the Germanna Plank Road, Stanhope took his men north on the Carolina Road that led across Mountain Run to Brandy Station. If he had gone just five miles west, he would have run into Longstreet's infantry corps of the Army of Northern Virginia. It was camped at the foot of Mount Pony. Before long he did see an oncoming Confederate cavalry column crossing Mountain Run on the road to Stevensburg. He beat a fast retreat back to the village. Stanhope informed Duffie of the Confederate presence. The Frenchman in return sent word to Stanhope to hold Stevensburg "at all hazards," that is, hold it to the bitter end. Perversely, he also ordered the major "if pushed too hard, to retreat slowly." While he may have expected trouble, Duffie did not increase the speed of his column as it followed Stanhope's wake.

Lieutenant Alexander Pennington, whose battery supported Duffie, is seen here on the far right. The gun is a 3in. Ordnance Rifle, such as used by all the Union artillery at Brandy Station. (Library of Congress)

Hansbrough Ridge, here looking west, was a formidable defensive position if held by enough men. Its height here can be measured by the six-foot-tall entrance sign to a farm. The old road ran approximately past the sign and parallel to the fence. (photo by Peggy Beattie)

RIGHT
Looking west along Kirtley Road, the main street of Stevensburg. Though the town is mostly hidden by trees, it is no larger than during the Civil War; this view is close to what Duffie saw from the church knoll. Mount Pony is five miles distant. (Photo by Peggy Beattie)

While these events occurred, Gregg led his 3rd Division and its battery at a gallop until the head of the division reached the rear of Duffie's column. Pleasonton had sent Gregg word by courier that he was badly needed, that Buford's wing was facing all of Stuart's cavalry. Gregg ordered his division to turn right onto the Fredericksburg Plank Road and proceed with care toward Brandy Station, less than five miles away. Gregg might well have suspected that he would show up behind Stuart with a full division of Union cavalry. He would find that he needed more.

Stuart knew of the crossing at Kelly's Ford early that morning and apparently assumed that the Union forces did not intend a major effort there.

He sent the 1st South Carolina Cavalry in that direction, then he relieved that regiment with Beverly Robertson's North Carolina Brigade with a section of guns. Robertson took the Old Carolina Road over Fleetwood Hill and traveled toward Norman's Ford on the Rappahannock. Short of the ford, another road, on the right, led to the small community of Kellysville and Kelly's Ford. Not far down that road, at the old battleground of March, Robertson ran into blue-coated infantry, cavalry and artillery. He dismounted most of the men in his two green regiments and sent mounted scouts to the flanks. The scouts reported three amazing pieces of information. First, there were large numbers of Union infantry ahead; second, they were slowly heading for Brandy Station; third, many Union cavalry were heading east to Madden's Tavern and possibly then to Stevensburg.

Robertson relayed this news to Stuart, near the Gee House. That the road to Madden's Tavern led eastward to Germanna and Ely's Fords and not directly to Stevensburg, and that there was a direct road to Stevensburg did not seem to occur to Robertson. If he had sent out his scouts again, Robertson might have learned that the Union cavalry rode not toward the tavern, but toward the town. The Confederate commander did not send parties to obstruct the Union troops by cutting down trees across the road; nor did he send observers to shadow the enemy cavalry column. Robertson apparently thought his job of watching the Union infantry advance up the Kelly's Ford–Brandy Station road and retiring slowly before them stretched his resources enough. Later he argued that Stuart had ordered him to "hold his front" and

Mountain Run near the site where Butler was wounded and Farley killed. While only a dozen feet across here, its steep banks made it a significant military obstacle. (Photo by Peggy Beattie)

he had obeyed the order as literally as he could. Around 9am, a messenger from "Grumble" Jones approached Stuart with information that some of the Union troops might enter Brandy Station from the south. "Tell General Jones to attend the Yankees in his front, and I'll watch the flanks," Stuart sarcastically informed the courier. Jones exploded with anger on receiving the retort, and grumbled, "So he thinks they ain't coming, does he? Well, let him alone; he'll damn soon see for himself."

Butler's stand

The Confederate cavalry that entered Stevensburg and vainly tried to catch Stanhope's men were the 2nd South Carolina Cavalry. They were few in number—perhaps 190 men—but led by a brave officer, Colonel Matthew Calbraith Butler. Butler's scouts soon informed him that he was greatly outnumbered as Duffie had at least 1,500 cavalry as well as an artillery battery. Even so, Butler decided to make a fight of it. He dismounted his men across the road, on the eastern slope of Hansbrough Ridge. A thin belt of trees ran north–south between the Hansbrough House and the Doggett House. Using trees and buildings to disguise his scant numbers, Butler hoped he could delay the enemy until expected reinforcements could bolster his defense. Stuart had earlier placed the 2nd South Carolina Cavalry of Hampton's Brigade, the 4th Virginia Cavalry of Munford's Brigade, and one gun in reserve in Brandy Station. Stuart's foresight would now pay dividends. The veteran 4th Virginia Cavalry had nearly 600 men, making it one of the largest units in the Cavalry Division, and Butler expected it to arrive soon.

Duffie attempted to measure the size and extent of the line opposing him. Mounted skirmishers ventured forward. They discovered that many of the South Carolinians had Enfield rifles, which greatly outranged their own carbines and forced them back. Duffie may have guessed how few Confederates were on the scene, or perhaps his men grew impatient. Ordered or not, Colonel Luigi di Cesnola's Brigade, led by the small 1st Massachusetts Cavalry, charged down the road toward the Confederate right. The local Confederate commander, Lieutenant-Colonel Frank Hampton, quickly ordered his three dozen troopers to their horses when he saw the sabers of a Union brigade bearing down on him. The men of the 1st Massachusetts, 6th Ohio, and 1st Rhode Island cavalry crashed into the scrambling Confederates. Numerous melees broke out along the road and on the grounds of the nearby 18th-century mansion named Salubria. They were brief fights: Hampton's men on the right were swamped and their commander, the brother of Wade Hampton, fell mortally wounded. The Union troopers pursued the running Confederates down the road and crashed into the 4th Virginia Cavalry. The latter regiment was unprepared for the onslaught as it had just emerged onto the road from a track through a pine forest, and was deploying from column of fours into a combat formation. It offered no resistance and the Virginians bolted westward toward the court house. "It was a regular steeple chase," remarked one of Duffie's men, "through ditches, over fences, through underbrush." Many Confederates did not rally until they reached a friendly battery hastily unlimbered by Longstreet at the foot of Mount Pony.

With his right flank gone, Butler could hold his line no longer. He retreated over Hansbrough Ridge toward Mountain Run. His left, under Major Thomas Lipscomb, however, did not see him leave or perhaps did not get the order to retire. Lipscomb's group escaped the attentions of the Union

forces at first and then escaped a hot pursuit. Duffie trotted his men into Stevensburg and continued north on the road to Brandy Station. From the church knoll he could see that there was fighting on Fleetwood Hill. He was within a mile of Mountain Run, which was three miles from Brandy Station. Blocking the way was the run itself, a narrow stream with steep banks, and an unknown number of Confederates (actually about 200 South Carolinians and Virginians) under Butler and one Confederate gun. While he pondered, his artillery commander, Lieutenant Alexander Pennington, positioned a section of his battery on a grassy hill. Pennington kept up a desultory duel with the Confederate field gun. Either one round went astray or Pennington switched targets. A projectile ripped through a small group of mounted Confederate officers. It nearly tore off Butler's right foot, penetrated his mount, passed through the adjacent horse of scout Will Farley, and cut off Farley's right leg at the knee. Farley was evacuated and died that evening. An ambulance carried Butler to surgeons, who amputated his foot. Soon after the command fell to him, Major Lipscomb led his men west to avoid the Union troops now to his rear in Brandy Station.

About noon, a staff officer from Gregg drew up in front of Duffie. Gregg ordered his subordinate to retrace his steps on the Kelly's Ford Road and join Gregg in Brandy Station. Slowly but with precision, Duffie took this roundabout route to Brandy Station with his two brigades, which had suffered some three dozen casualties so far. By the time his tired troopers covered the six miles to Gregg, the fighting was over around the town of Brandy Station. Much blood had been shed in the interim for possession of Fleetwood Hill.

The last stage of a cavalry charge, when the horses are in full career. (*Marshall's Crossroads*, courtesy of Keith Rocco)

The town of Brandy Station as seen from the site of Major McClellan's position near Stuart's former headquarters. The three trees in the middle distance, at the bottom of the slope, mark the course of Flat Run. A bit of the Old Carolina Road can be seen at the far right. (Photo by Peggy Beattie)

THE FIGHT FOR FLEETWOOD HILL

In contrast to the excitement at dawn on Fleetwood Hill and the fighting elsewhere that morning, Brandy Station, Fleetwood Hill and the mile of meadow in between were placid at mid-morning. Butler had sent a 30-man detail of the 2nd South Carolina Cavalry south to watch the road that ran past Carrico's Mill. Then he took the rest of his regiment west to Stevensburg, followed by the 4th Virginia Cavalry. No soldiers or military activity were left in this, the Confederate rear area, except wagons taking wounded to the rear or ammunition to the front, the walking wounded and a small group of men on the hill. Stuart had left on the site of his former headquarters a trusted staff officer along with couriers to forward dispatches. Some signalmen nearby maintained flag contact with army headquarters at the courthouse via another signal post on Mount Pony. The officer here, Stuart's assistant adjutant-general or chief clerk, was Major Henry B. McClellan. While new to the staff, McClellan was prized for his intelligence and dedication. That he was a native Pennsylvanian and first cousin to George B. McClellan, former commander of the enemy army, was not held against him. Stuart would soon have reason to celebrate McClellan's cool courage.

At about 10.30am a feverish rider, one of Robertson's officers, pelted up the hill and blurted out to McClellan that the Union cavalry that had crossed at Kelly's Ford were now approaching the southern outskirts of Brandy Station. How could they have got around Robertson? Perhaps the scout had mistaken Butler's riders on the Carrico's Mill Road for the enemy. McClellan needed verification and told him to go and check again. The North Carolinian returned a few minutes later, now insisting that McClellan could see for

LEFT
A photograph from the early spring of 1864 that shows Brandy Station when it was the main supply depot for the wintering Army of the Potomac. The station is on the left and above it, a mile away, Fleetwood Hill. (Library of Congress)

BELOW
Fleetwood Hill as seen from the second position of Martin's Battery. Stuart's headquarters was about where the shed is, the Miller House a bit to the left of that. (Photo by Peggy Beattie)

himself. The Carrico's Mill Road was bordered by a heavy growth of trees. Short of the town the trees disappeared and exposed the road. And into this large clearing was now pouring a column of horsemen in dark blue, with cavalry guidons in the stars and stripes pattern, and vedettes fanning out ahead. In their probe south, Butler's party of scouts had ridden past the disused Fredericksburg Plank Road that joined the Mill Road below the town. They continued south as Gregg's column came north. Gregg's outriders skillfully snapped up a few Confederate sentries without any warning being given.

How could the Union forces be prevented from seizing not only the town, but also the key terrain of Fleetwood Hill? In control of the heights, they would be only a mile from the Confederate line at St. James Church. McClellan sent a courier to warn his superior. As he wrote later: "Matters seemed serious!" In one of his glances rearward, McClellan spotted a single Confederate field gun 100 yards east, at the foot of the hill. Lieutenant John W. Carter of Chew's Ashby Artillery commanded the gun, later identified by McClellan as a 6-pdr howitzer, but more likely it was a 12-pdr Napoleon

SAVE THE DAY! (pp. 68–69)

About 10.30am, Gregg's Division of Union cavalry appeared two miles behind Stuart's main line of battle at St. James Church. The key terrain of Fleetwood Hill lay in between and was almost empty of Confederate troops. Fortunately for Stuart, one of them was Major Henry B. McClellan, Stuart's assistant adjutant general (**1**). McClellan was new to Stuart's staff, but he performed splendidly now. McClellan sent couriers to alert Stuart and ordered a nearby cannon to mount the hill, unlimber, and fire slowly on the Union troops. At about 11am, the lead brigade of Gregg's force, led by Colonel Percy Wyndham started to advance on the hill. About 900 Union horsemen were about to sieze the key terrain on the battlefield without a struggle. They threatened to attack Stuart's two brigades engaged at St. James Church in the rear.

Glancing to the rear, McClellan saw Confederate cavalry approaching in column, the 12th Virginia Cavalry of Jones's Brigade (**2**), which had seen heavy action already this day. Since they were trotting forward with deliberation, McClellan raced down from the hill to plead the urgency of the situation.

Colonel Asher Harman (**3**) ordered his troopers to charge the crest of the hill without taking the time to deploy from column of fours. The unit was led by Company B, the Baylor Light Cavalry. Harman at the very front had around himself barely two dozen of his Shenandoah Valley men, including, on his right, his younger brother Lt. Louis Harman (**4**), the regiment's adjutant. Even so, he shouted "Charge," which one of his men said was his favorite and virtually the only order he knew. Harman's men clambered up the gentle slope and pitched into the Federal cavalry, who had nearly gained the crest. The Confederates did not succeed in stopping their enemies, but they did delay them. Harman was badly wounded later in the day by a saber cut in the continuing fight for Fleetwood Hill but survived the battle. A month later he was captured and remained a prisoner nearly to the end of the war. McClellan would always regret that the sacrifice of many brave men in the 12th Virginia was necessary to save the day.

gun-howitzer. Just why it was there is unknown, but what matters is that McClellan brought it up to his location on the lawn of the Miller House. He told Carter to open a slow fire upon the distant enemy cavalry, and then he sent more gallopers to alert Stuart.

The booming of the single artillery piece disconcerted Sir Percy Wyndham. Perhaps the Confederates wanted the gun to appear vulnerable in order to lure the Union troops into a trap. Perhaps more guns and Confederates were hidden in the trees around the white house on the hill. Only a few men were visible on Fleetwood Hill, which stretched over two miles northward. A prudent commander weighs possibilities and Wyndham sent an aide back to notify Gregg, his divisional commander. Then he hastily deployed his brigade south of the town, facing Fleetwood Hill. He had three units: the 1st New Jersey Cavalry, the 1st Pennsylvania Cavalry and the small 1st Maryland Cavalry. He called up Lieutenant Moses Clark's section of the 6th New York Independent Battery that had accompanied his brigade. Clark put them in position on a grassy rise just south of the railroad tracks and they opened fire to reconnoiter what was truly on the hill.

At St. James Church, Stuart was surprised but not alarmed by the news brought by McClellan's first courier. This new messenger came up soon after that annoying warning from Jones. Surely this was some error; Stuart could not believe that he had been tricked a second time. He summoned Captain Hart, most of whose Blakely cannons had cracked their carriages and were temporarily unusable. "Ride back there and see what this foolishness is about," he barked to Hart. That officer was still in sight when a clerk from Stuart's headquarters reined in and shouted, "General, the Yankees are at Brandy." Stuart reacted fast. He ordered Jones to send his two closest units, the 12th Virginia Cavalry and the 35th Virginia Cavalry Battalion, to the town. Since Jones had already detached the 7th Virginia Cavalry to "Rooney" Lee and the 6th Virginia Cavalry were still with Hampton, that left Jones in charge of a single regiment, the 11th Virginia Cavalry. Stuart also ordered Hampton to send one regiment, and he released the 6th Virginia Cavalry, while Beckham sent a section of horse artillery.

The Miller House on Fleetwood Hill during the autumn of 1863, looking north. The artist has dramatically diminished the size of the soldiers marching along the embankment of the Orange & Alexandria Railroad. Flat Run flows under the culvert. (Photo courtesy Virginia Historical Society, Richmond, Virginia)

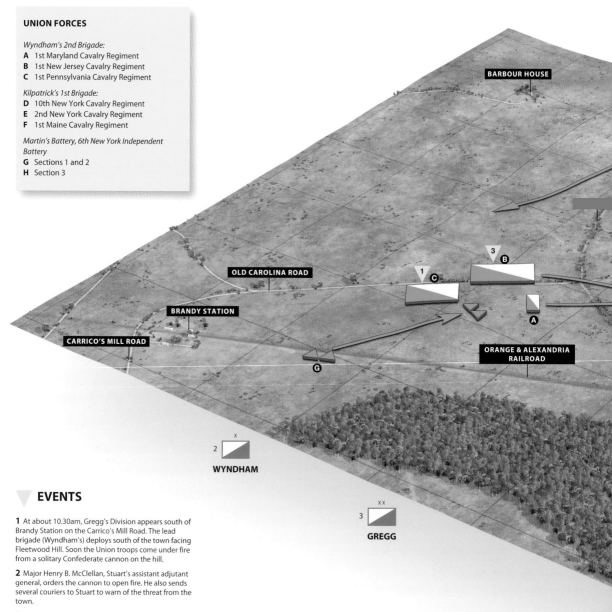

BARBOUR HOUSE

OLD CAROLINA ROAD

BRANDY STATION

CARRICO'S MILL ROAD

ORANGE & ALEXANDRIA RAILROAD

2 WYNDHAM

3 GREGG

▼ EVENTS

1 At about 10.30am, Gregg's Division appears south of Brandy Station on the Carrico's Mill Road. The lead brigade (Wyndham's) deploys south of the town facing Fleetwood Hill. Soon the Union troops come under fire from a solitary Confederate cannon on the hill.

2 Major Henry B. McClellan, Stuart's assistant adjutant general, orders the cannon to open fire. He also sends several couriers to Stuart to warn of the threat from the town.

3 At about 11.00am, Wyndham's Brigade starts to move up the hill with two sections of Martin's Battery assisting the advance.

4 Wyndham's Brigade nearly reaches the crest of the hill when its lead unit, the 1st Maryland, is hit by the 12th Virginia. A protracted melee erupts that soon includes the 35th Virginia Battalion and the 6th Virginia. Wyndham retires towards the town about noon.

5 The second Union brigade, under Kilpatrick, attempts to attack the hill from the south in echelon formation. The 10th New York and 2nd New York retreat after being hit in the flank by the Cobb's Legion and the 1st South Carolina. The 1st Maine, the last of Kilpatrick's regiments, storms the hill, bypassing the Georgia and South Carolina horsemen. The Maine troopers disperse the 6th Virginia on the top of the hill, ride around both sides of the Miller House complex, and overrun the Confederate artillery.

6 With blown horses, the 1st Maine returns south of the tracks. They do not attack the Barbour House where Generals Robert E. Lee and Richard Ewell are watching the struggle for Fleetwood Hill.

7 The newly arrived 11th Virginia travels west on the Old Carolina Road and overruns Martin's Union Battery. They then pursue Wyndham's troopers to the edge of town until halted by accidental fire from the re-manned Confederate artillery.

8 The 1st North Carolina and the Jeff Davis Legion capture many of Kilpatrick's soldiers, who are reforming south of the tracks. These Confederate regiments, led by Hampton himself, aim for the town. They are also halted by mistaken Confederate artillery fire. The fighting on this part of the field ends at about 1.30pm.

THE FIGHT FOR FLEETWOOD HILL, JUNE 9, 1863
Major McClellan saves the day

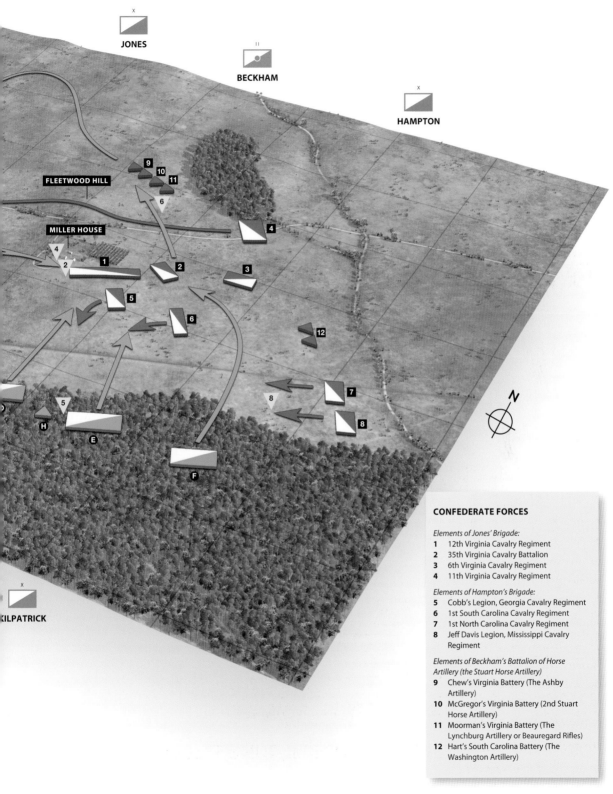

Note: Gridlines are shown at intervals of 250 yds/228m

JONES

BECKHAM

HAMPTON

FLEETWOOD HILL

9
10 11
6
4

MILLER HOUSE

4
2 1 2 3

5
6

12

7

8

5
H
E
8

F

N

KILPATRICK

CONFEDERATE FORCES

Elements of Jones' Brigade:
1　12th Virginia Cavalry Regiment
2　35th Virginia Cavalry Battalion
3　6th Virginia Cavalry Regiment
4　11th Virginia Cavalry Regiment

Elements of Hampton's Brigade:
5　Cobb's Legion, Georgia Cavalry Regiment
6　1st South Carolina Cavalry Regiment
7　1st North Carolina Cavalry Regiment
8　Jeff Davis Legion, Mississippi Cavalry Regiment

Elements of Beckham's Battalion of Horse Artillery (the Stuart Horse Artillery)
9　Chew's Virginia Battery (The Ashby Artillery)
10　McGregor's Virginia Battery (2nd Stuart Horse Artillery)
11　Moorman's Virginia Battery (The Lynchburg Artillery or Beauregard Rifles)
12　Hart's South Carolina Battery (The Washington Artillery)

Meanwhile the Union threat to Fleetwood had become greater. The artillery section of Martin's Battery suppressed the Confederate gun within fifteen minutes, though a round got stuck in the bore of one of the Union guns, disabling it. Gregg ordered Captain Joseph Martin to bring up his second section and have all three guns move closer to the hill to support an advance by Wyndham's brigade. Martin had some difficulty getting his guns and teams over the high railroad embankment, and Wyndham's advance had already begun. Martin dropped the trails of his guns about halfway to the crest of the hill. On top of the hill, Lieutenant Carter withdrew his gun after emptying his limber-chest of ammunition. Gregg saw this movement as an opportunity to take the hill and told Wyndham the time was ripe.

Wyndham himself led the 1st New Jersey Cavalry, its alignment guided by the Old Carolina Road. It was in a column of squadrons that was perhaps 24 men wide (28 yards) and 12 men deep (perhaps 100 yards), with Wyndham riding in front. To its right rode two squadrons from the 1st Maryland Cavalry, while to their right came the 1st Pennsylvania Cavalry, in a formation like that of their New Jersey comrades but larger. The brigade hesitated briefly at a rivulet called Flat Run at the foot of the hill. Then the 900 or so cavalrymen began the ascent. Major McClellan watched uneasily their measured approach; he also looked to the east for help. When he first saw the column of Colonel Asher Harman's 12th Virginia Cavalry, he feared his rescuers were coming on far too leisurely as Harman's column of fours was moving at a trot. McClellan galloped up to Harman to plead the urgency of the situation and Harman and his regiment, well strung out with the faster horses pushing to the front, swept up the gentle slope, over the crest and past the Miller House. Harman at the very front had around himself barely two dozen of his Shenandoah Valley men and, even so, shouted "Charge." The 1st Maryland Cavalry was nearly at the crest when Harman's group came down the slope and pitched into them. The Virginians shattered like spray against the bow of a battleship, according to one Union trooper. The rest of Harman's Regiment arrived on the hilltop without bothering to deploy. Many Union troops arrived too; the 1st Maryland Cavalry reached the crest first, then the 1st Pennsylvania Cavalry and the New Jersey regiment. Even one gun of Martin's horse artillery made it to the top of the hill and fired a few rounds, though its crew soon recognized their peril and withdrew. The Union force compelled the 12th Virginia Cavalry to fall back in disorder and Harman withdrew his men off the hill to rally, but some of them collided with the 35th Virginia Cavalry Battalion as it approached. The 35th quickly disentangled itself from Harman's Regiment and joined the fray. It split to attack around both sides of the Miller House. "There now followed a passage of arms filled with romantic interest and splendor to a degree unequaled by anything our war produced," penned a staff officer under Stuart. The battle here had come down to a fierce melee filled with sounds of clanging sabers, blazing pistol shots and the screams of hurt horses. The choking dust and hair from the swirling horses blinded the soldiers. One Maryland trooper remembered it made it difficult to tell "t'other from which." The garden, orchard and cabins next to the house disrupted formations. Finally the southern end of Fleetwood Hill fell into a lull as the 35th Virginia Cavalry Battalion retired east and the drained men and panting horses of both sides tried to re-form. Two officers on opposite sides of the hill reacted differently to the situation. Stuart left the reordering of his two units to others and went back to get the rest of the brigades left near St. James Church. Near the town, Gregg saw his men apparently in control of what he called "the coveted hill." He "showed an enthusiasm that I had never noticed before," noted his adjutant. Gregg started toward the hill, swinging his gauntlets and hurrahing. But he was focused enough to order an aide to hasten the approach of his other brigade, Kilpatrick's, into the fight. About this time, he decided he needed reinforcements and sent a courier to tell Duffie to join him at Brandy Station.

The respite from carnage on the hill was brief: the 12th and the 35th came back for more, joined by several hundred men of the 6th Virginia Cavalry. The latter regiment drove the New Jersey troopers from around the house and continued down the hill against the three guns of Martin's Battery. Canister could not stop the Confederates, though one of the badly wounded was Lieutenant R. O. Allen, the man who had killed "Grimes" Davis. In the fierce free-for-all, the artillery crews and drivers fought back with pistols and artillery implements. Some gunners crouched under the gun carriages. Some Union cavalrymen came to their assistance. "They were the bravest cannoneers that ever followed a gun," admitted one of the Virginians. "As we shot their men and horses down, they would fight us with their swabs, with but few of them left." Having apparently crippled the battery and now threatened with encirclement, the Confederates climbed back up the hill. Closely followed by the Union cavalry, they panicked and stampeded off the crest. Soon after the retreat of the 6th Virginia Cavalry, the 35th Virginia Cavalry Battalion spied some of Martin's men still serving their guns and darted at them. Another brawl broke out around the three field pieces. The ground there was already littered with blue and gray casualties and the carcasses of horses.

After an hour or so of fighting on the hill, charging and countercharging, the troopers of Wyndham's Brigade were exhausted and their horses blown. Key officers were down, including the commander of the 1st New Jersey Cavalry and others. Companies, squadrons and regiments were intermingled. Wyndham's troops fell back down the western slope of the hill about the same time that Kilpatrick's fresh brigade stormed the southern tip.

Kilpatrick had led his cavalry brigade, still in column of fours, east and parallel to the tracks by an old road. The third section of Martin's Battery followed them. Trees hid their movement from enemy sight. Gregg intended that they should deploy once they had got southeast of the hill, cross the railroad embankment and tracks, and strike against the heights. Kilpatrick planned to attack "en echelon," each regiment in a column of squadrons. From west to east they formed up in a belt of timber opposite Fleetwood Hill, the 10th New York Cavalry, the 2nd New York Cavalry and the 1st Maine Cavalry. An attack in echelon, the 10th leading, then the other two units attacking from left to right, would help protect the right flank of the brigade from attackers. The formation was not out of the ordinary, but its execution here was disastrous. The 10th led off the advance and, after emerging from the woods, they crossed an open space until they came to some swampy ground and the embankment, tracks, drainage ditches and a fence that marked the course of the Orange & Alexandria Railroad. These obstacles compelled the regiment to halt and re-form on the north side of the tracks. Bugles signaled the advance and, the gait of the horses increasing, the regiment thrust up the hill. They were accompanied by Lieutenant Wade Wilson's section of Martin's Battery, which with difficulty had negotiated the obstacles at the tracks. Suddenly a torrent of horsemen crying the Rebel yell hit the regiment on its right.

Major Henry B. McClellan, a former ministry student and schoolteacher, had been on Stuart's staff only a few weeks at the time of the battle. (Photo courtesy of Clark B. Hall)

The 35th Virginia Cavalry Battalion, led by Lieutenant-Colonel Elijah White on the gray horse, overruns Martin's 6th New York Independent Battery. Brandy Station is on the far right. In 1864, White's unit would gain the nickname "The Gray Comanches." (*The Gray Comanches*, painting by Don Troiani, www.historicalimagebank.com)

Back near the town, Gregg had seen through the dust those same gray riders approaching fast and in good order. He assumed they were part of Buford's Wing coming to his support. They actually were following the orders of Hampton and Stuart. Hampton had anticipated the need to head for the town and had decided that the situation demanded that he not wait for his dismounted skirmishers to come back to their held horses and reassemble. Leaving them to catch up later, he sent the bulk of Cobb's Legion of Georgians, Alabamians and Mississippians, as well as the 1st South Carolina Cavalry, immediately southwestward. Having seen them off, he personally led the 1st North Carolina Cavalry and the Jeff Davis Legion of Mississippians toward the tracks. Captain Hart of the Washington Artillery had patched together one of his disabled Blakelys and he brought it and another along. Before long, the rest of Beckham's Battalion limbered up and dashed for Fleetwood Hill, following the 11th Virginia Cavalry and Jones, who had been summoned by Stuart. Jones in turn ordered the 7th Virginia Cavalry to leave "Rooney" Lee and come to southern Fleetwood Hill. Stuart also diverted Hampton's first two regiments and told them to remove the Union forces from the hill.

It was one of these units, Cobb's Legion, that hit the flank of the 10th New York Cavalry. The 1st South Carolina Cavalry followed Cobb's Legion closely.

Hart's guns unlimbered at close range to assist these cavalry. Although Wilson had put his two Union guns into position to fire also, he could not find a good target before Confederate horsemen overran him. Although Union troopers intervened to save his guns, Kilpatrick saw that Wilson's artillery section was increasingly isolated and ordered it to fall back. Wilson swiftly brought his section back over the tracks and ditches. It was a nerve-racking retreat that included one of the limbers overturning until righted by those gunners not engaged in fighting off enemy horsemen. After a scrimmage on the slope, Cobb's Legion chased the 10th New York Cavalry off the hill and back to the woods south of the tracks. Many Union troopers were killed or captured when their horses balked at crossing the ditches next to the tracks.

Kilpatrick's echelon formation had failed to prevent the enemy attack from the east because the next unit in line, the 2nd New York Cavalry, had been delayed. Its lead squadron misheard an order and wheeled 90 degrees to the left after crossing the tracks. Thus it advanced on the town rather than Fleetwood Hill. The regimental commander adjusted the course of his unit just in time for it to be flanked by the 1st South Carolina Cavalry. "They fired on us and fled," recalled one of the Southern attackers, "never attempting to stand the shock." Kilpatrick had once commanded the 2nd New York Cavalry, nicknamed the Harris Light Cavalry. Now, under Kilpatrick's gaze, they fought briefly and routed back to the woods south of the tracks. The first two regiments of Kilpatrick's brigade had "floated off as feathers on a wind," according to Kilpatrick. The brigade commander then galloped over to the Colonel Alvin Doughty of the 1st Maine Cavalry. This regiment had been slow to cross the tracks also. Though many in its ranks were unlikely material for cavalrymen—former fishermen, mechanics and lumberjacks—the 1st Maine Cavalry was eager to launch their first charge of the war. "Colonel Doughty, what can you do with your regiment?" roared Kilpatrick. The reply: "I can drive the Rebels to Hell, Sir!" Some also remembered Kilpatrick beseeching, "Men of Maine, you must save the day!"

Then the 1st Maine Cavalry launched one of the great saber charges of the war. Riding with its colonel was Lieutenant R. B. Porter, who felt a rush of excitement: "Who can describe the feelings of a man on entering a charge? How exhilarating, and yet how awful. The glory of success in a charge is intoxicating! One forgets everything, even personal safety, in the one grand thought of vanquishing the enemy. We were in for it now, and the nerves were strung to the highest tension." They spurred up the hill behind the first two of Hampton's regiments, ignored them and plowed into the 6th Virginia Cavalry. Once again the 6th ran and the Union troopers split around the Miller House complex (house, barn, slave cabins, garden and orchard) and continued northward along the ridge. Now it was the turn of the Confederate artillery, in battery north of the house to be overrun. There was furious and brief combat among the guns. One of the men of McGregor's Battery could later boast that he had knocked one Union trooper out the saddle with a rammer and captured him. After many of the artillerists abandoned their guns, the Maine troopers continued north along the west slope of the hill. Their impetus carried them a mile, close to the Barbour House, named "Beauregard." Perhaps they were not close enough to the grounds of the house to see the crowd of tethered horses belonging to General Robert E. Lee, General Richard Ewell and their staffs. The army commander and the leader of 2nd Corps had heard the noise from the battlefield and had come out from the courthouse to get a look at the battle from only a half-mile away. They were probably in the cupola as the unknowing 1st Maine Cavalry hurdled by. The Maine warriors finally turned around and cut their way back the way they had come, or found alternative routes to safety across the railroad tracks. In addition to the tale of their wild ride, they brought trophies. Some men remembered Kilpatrick demanding possession of a captured Rebel flag. The captor pointed out that there were others up on the hill, and if the colonel "wanted one bad, he had better go out and get one for himself."

Hampton meanwhile crossed to the southeast side of the tracks and pushed westward across the fields adjacent to the woods with the 1st North Carolina Cavalry and the Jeff Davis Legion. His men gathered in many jaded prisoners from Kilpatrick's Brigade. They might have attacked the feeble defenders of the town if Confederate artillery had not opened fire through the dust on Hampton's flank and driven him back. Hampton was enraged that the Confederate artillery denied him the full fruits of victory. Although few Union troops still contested ownership of Fleetwood Hill, the final charge that crowned the day was delivered by the 11th Virginia Cavalry. Directed by Stuart and Jones, they poured over the hill by the Old Carolina Road. On the west side of the hill they attacked the few remaining, bedraggled men of Martin's artillery. The Confederates easily rode down the dismounted Maryland cavalrymen supposedly supporting the cannons though Martin's survivors of two earlier overruns this day still fought hard. With his artillery horses mostly dead or wounded, Martin made the hardest decision an artilleryman can make: to abandon his guns. He made his way back to the town with six unwounded men out of the 36 in his two sections that had fired on Fleetwood Hill from the west. Martin later reported of the behavior of his men: "Not one of them flinched for a moment from his duty." The same could be said of Wilson's section, which operated with Kilpatrick and returned with all their guns.

The 11th Virginia Cavalry had the honor of participating in the last of the fighting. They drove Wyndham's tired Union troopers to the town, where the 11th also came under fire from the Confederate guns on Fleetwood Hill. Stuart sent squadrons of this regiment to check the roads west to Stevensburg and Culpeper Court House for Union stragglers. During the retreat Sir Percy took a bullet in his calf and only after putting his command in good order, did he pass command to a subordinate several hours later and go to a surgeon. After the head of Duffie's Division appeared from the south to protect Gregg's men, Stuart called an end to the pursuit. He had no reserves except Robertson's inexperienced men who along with the 7th Virginia Cavalry had just joined Stuart at Fleetwood Hill. Undoubtedly Stuart decided to hold onto his hard-won repossession of the dominant terrain. It was probably no later than 1.30pm when the fury on the hill ended. Confederates went to the rear with prisoners or rejoined their own regiments, sometimes with new horses or weapons in hand. Except for bugles sounding "Assembly," the moans of the wounded, and shots dispatching badly wounded horses, the hill, the plain and the town were at peace again.

PLEASONTON ORDERS THE RETREAT

Gregg contacted Pleasonton about 1.00pm to inform the corps commander that his division was used up. He accurately reported that his division had been outnumbered all day, but he also told Pleasonton that Confederate infantry had advanced by train close to Brandy Station: reason enough for his

The Orange & Alexandria Railroad Bridge and Cow's Ford on the Rappahannock River near Rappahannock Station. Culpeper County is to the left, Fauquier County to the right. Gregg's Division and Russell's infantry retreated over the river here. (Library of Congress)

cavalry to fall back. Apparently Gregg made up the story of the enemy infantry as there is no corroborating evidence. Lee had ordered two brigades of Ewell's infantry to march to Botts's Estate earlier in the day, as insurance in case Stuart was beaten. But it is very unlikely that Gregg meant these troops as they were over two miles away. By 1863, the bogus threat of infantry intervening in a cavalry battle was a standard excuse for cavalry to retreat. The same excuse was used at Kelly's Ford, Trevilian Station and at several other battles besides Brandy Station.

Without fresh troops Pleasonton thought it fruitless to attempt another effort against Fleetwood Hill. He had not sent Devin's cavalry and Ames's infantry into the fighting at Fleetwood Hill after 11am, when most of Stuart's soldiers had left their line at St. James Church. Duffie's Division was exhausted, from lack of sleep rather than combat, and probably not capable of effective fighting. Neither Pleasonton nor Gregg bothered ordering Russell's untouched infantry brigade and artillery battery to the heart of the battle.

Gregg led his division without incident to the river opposite Rappahannock Station, where they crossed to safety by ford and railroad bridge. Duffie's Division skillfully covered this movement, repeated their rearguard duties on Buford's front, and finally crossed to Fauquier County at Beverly Ford in the early evening. Russell's men also crossed at Rappahannock Station, and Sweitzer's Brigade returned to Kelly's Ford. The lack of any enemy pursuit reveals that the Confederates had also endured a trying day in Culpeper County.

The Confederate battle flag, however, and not the Stars and Stripes, waved in triumph among the debris of battle on Fleetwood Hill that evening. Although some partisans at the time, and since, have called the battle of Brandy Station

The Barbour House, "Beauregard," from the edge of the town. During the Civil War the house had a cupola. A little of Fleetwood Hill can be seen on the right. (Photo by Peggy Beattie)

a draw or even a Union victory, it was neither. It was a marginal Confederate victory. In their after-action reports, both commanders magnified their successes and downplayed their failures. Nowhere in his report on "the battle of Fleetwood" does Stuart use the word "surprise." He praised Hampton, Jones and especially "Rooney" Lee, the wounded son of his superior officer. He pointed out that Robertson and Munford had each made a serious error: Robertson by missing Gregg's approach to the Confederate rear, Munford for excessive tardiness. Stuart explained that he had planned all along to make "the real stand" on Fleetwood Hill and that he had meant to keep his troops concentrated "to strike him with my whole force." It would not have sounded so well had he said that the enemy came close to surrounding the "concentrated" cavalry of Lee's army. Undoubtedly caught off guard twice, Stuart responded to the various crises of the battle with vigor and tactical acumen. One soldier recalled that he was " Here, there and everywhere … ringing out the words of command." And his men fought superbly.

True to form, Pleasonton claimed victory in the "battle of Beverly Ford" and threw in a few choice lies to reinforce his assertion. According to him, despite two to one odds, he had crippled Stuart's cavalry and decisively prevented Stuart's planned raid. After all, he had captured Stuart's headquarters with important, revealing papers. Only the advent of Confederate infantry had forced his withdrawal. None of that was true: not the odds, not the crippling, not the raid, not the headquarters, not key papers not Confederate infantry. Months later, after Gettysburg, he even boasted that he had uncovered Lee's plans to invade the North. In his report he, like Gregg, emphasized Duffie's incompetence. He crowed that his reconnaisssance in force had been successful. Pleasonton did not mention his actual orders from Hooker: to seek out and destroy Stuart's command. One truthful statement, though, shines out like a beacon from his account: "The troops are in splendid spirits and are entitled to the highest praise for their distinguished conduct."

The Union cavalry were proud that they had given as good as they got. Many Confederates were astonished that the until-now-contemptible Union horsemen had fought so well. One private of the 6th Virginia Cavalry wrote that they "exhibited marked and wonderful improvement in skill, confidence, and tenacity." A Confederate hero of the battle, Major Henry B. McClellan, later wrote:

> One result of incalculable importance certainly did follow this battle,—it made the Federal cavalry. Up to that time confessedly inferior to the Southern horsemen, they gained on this day the confidence in themselves and their commanders which enabled them to contest so fiercely the subsequent battlefields of June, July, and October.

The casualties of Brandy Station cannot be pinned down precisely. The Confederates probably lost about 600 killed, wounded, missing, and captured. The Union forces probably lost about 900 and Martin's three cannon. Of course, hundreds of horses perished. These are small numbers compared to the great bloodletting at Gettysburg three weeks later, where more than 46,000 men became casualties. But as the cavalrymen of both sides rode and fought in Virginia, Maryland and Pennsylvania over the next two years, they would remember with pride their deeds in the first battle of the Gettysburg campaign, Brandy Station.

ROADS TO GETTYSBURG

Though Stuart's command took six days to refit, Brandy Station did not delay the march of the rest of Lee's Army. On June 10, Ewell's Corps marched for Chester Gap in the Blue Ridge to gain access to the Shenandoah Valley. Lee sent Longstreet's Corps along the eastern slope of the Blue Ridge chain to befuddle Hooker. It was to cross to the valley via Ashby's Gap. Most of Stuart's troopers, once rested and refurbished, protected Longstreet's column. After Longstreet and A. P. Hill had entered the valley, Stuart was to guard the various gaps, or passes, of the Blue Ridge from the "eyes" of General Joseph Hooker. Lee wished the Union commander kept in doubt of his plans as long as possible.

The Union cavalry recuperated quickly from the battle The men and horses rested after their great efforts across the Rappahannock while the Cavalry Bureau supplied hundreds of remounts. The Quartermaster Department replaced ammunition, weapons, saddles and other gear. Hooker was satisfied with the state of his horsemen when he reviewed them at Catlett's Station on June 11. He reorganized them the same day; Buford was appointed permanent commander of the 1st Division, which now included the Reserve Brigade, Gregg was placed in command of a new 2nd Division, Duffie was reduced to regimental command and his old 2nd Division was broken up and its units divided between the other divisions. There was no longer a 3rd Division. Eleven days later, Pleasonton himself was confirmed as permanent commander of the Cavalry Corps and secured a second star for his "victory" at Brandy Station.

In mid-June, the Bureau of Military Information lost track of most of Lee's Army. Nor did Hooker know if any reinforcements had joined his enemy. Most important of all, Hooker did not know what Lee was up to. He turned to Pleasonton to find out but his cavalry commander seemed unable to discriminate between sundry bits of information procured from civilians, deserters, his cavalry, escaped slaves and his imagination. Once he ludicrously suggested that Lee meant to attack Pittsburgh in the mountains of western Pennsylvania.

More accurate news soon arrived from a distant battlefield. On June 14, Ewell's Corps, which had crossed the Blue Ridge into the Shenandoah Valley, struck at the Union garrisons in the lower Shenandoah: at Winchester, Martinsburg, and Berryville. At Stephenson's Depot, near Winchester, Ewell "gobbled up" (as Lincoln put it) more than half of the garrison of Winchester as it tried to escape. The Union forces also left all their supplies, wagons and artillery behind.

Harpers Ferry might be Lee's next target, and after that Washington or someplace north of the Potomac. The government demanded Hooker do something in response. Even before the bad news of Winchester reached the White House, Lincoln had dismissed Hooker's latest strategic scheme. Hooker desired to cross the Rappahannock, crush A. P. Hill's Confederates at Fredericksburg, and throw his army against lightly guarded Richmond. The President quickly and sharply dismissed Hooker's idea: "I think *Lee's* Army, and not *Richmond*, is your true objective point." Finally, through BMI intelligence rather than cavalry probes, Hooker learned that Lee was moving northwest with his whole army. Hooker may have seen the strategic light after receiving Lincoln's homely inquiry, "If the head of Lee's army is at Martinsburg and the tail of it on the Plank Road between Fredericksburg and Chancellorsville, the animal must be very slim somewhere. Could you not break him?" Hooker set his army in pursuit on June 13.

Three days later Hooker complained to Lincoln, "We can never discover the whereabouts of the enemy, or divine his intentions, so long as he fills the country with a cloud of cavalry. We must break through that to find him." This indirect slap at Pleasonton had considerable merit. The cavalry remained unskillful at gathering useful intelligence and seemed incapable of penetrating Stuart's screen. Pleasonton's ineptitude at reconnaissance was creating an intelligence fog for Hooker. The next day Hooker's chief of staff sent helpful advice to Pleasonton reminding him that the commanding general "relies upon you with your cavalry force to give him the information of where the enemy is, his force, and his movements. You have a sufficient cavalry force to do this. Drive in [his] pickets, if necessary, and get us information. It is better that we should lose men than to be without knowledge of the enemy, as we now seem to be." This message spurred Pleasonton to act promptly and decisively.

BATTLES FOR A BLUE RIDGE GAP

Between Washington and Hooker's army and the Blue Ridge barrier lay another, smaller mountain chain and north–south wall, the Bull Run Mountains. Between the two parallel chains lay a space a dozen miles in width called the Loudoun Valley. A well-traveled road bisected the valley east to west and split just west of the town of Aldie. The main road, the Ashby's Gap Turnpike, ran west, through Middleburg and Upperville, and climbed the Blue Ridge to Ashby's Gap. The lesser road led northwest to Snicker's Gap. While the beautiful Loudoun Valley was important strategically, its stone walls, streams and woods aided a defender. These features, and the absence of some of his brigades, convinced Stuart to fight defensively there. To Aldie, the Loudoun Valley and the strategic gaps rode Pleasonton's Corps in the third week of June. The Confederates were there already.

Three cavalry battles erupted. The first, on June 17, saw a brigade under newly promoted Judson Kilpatrick attack Munford's Virginia Brigade just beyond Aldie in what Stuart called one of the bloodiest engagements of the war. Both sides were surprised and, as at Brandy Station, Kilpatrick launched furious, piecemeal assaults. Again he was repulsed. Munford, nevertheless, fell back. Pleasonton had meanwhile sent the 1st Rhode Island Cavalry, Colonel Alfred Duffie commanding, to scout Middleburg. Duffie found Stuart there—almost capturing him—and a great many Confederate cavalry. Barricaded and surrounded in Middleburg, Duffie sent for help. Pleasonton sent none. Pleasonton had, however, somehow acquired enough news to notify Hooker that "From all the information I can gather, there was no force of consequence of the enemy's infantry this side of the Blue Ridge." Hooker wrote back that a cavalry leader was supposed to find where the enemy was, not where he wasn't. Pleasonton had actually discovered very little about the

whereabouts of the Confederates; he had even failed to locate Longstreet's 20,000 men at the eastern foot of the mountains, ten miles away. On the 19th, Pleasonton recapped the Aldie battle with another frontal assault along the Pike, five miles west at Middleburg. Gregg's Division did most of the fighting. It turned into another bloody, indecisive mix-up, with charges and countercharges alternating, though Stuart fell back in the end. After this brawl, Pleasonton informed his superior, "We cannot force the gaps of the Blue Ridge in the presence of a superior force." He requested infantry assistance to counter Stuart's effective use of dismounted skirmishers.

The last of the Loudoun Valley battles occurred on the 21st at Upperville, four miles west of Middleburg and at the very foot of the mountains. Pleasonton thought he had the answer to Stuart's effective tactics of placing horse artillery and dismounted cavalry behind stone walls and backing them up with mounted cavalry for counterattacks. The Union battle plan this time combined frontal attacks using both cavalry divisions to pin their enemy, supplemented by a brigade of Union infantry to outflank the enemy defenses. The new Union tactics produced much hand-to-hand fighting and some success. One Union infantry officer thought the sight magnificent: "the sabres flashed in the sun as the men mingled together and fought in a writhing mass, cutting and slashing each other. Riderless horses ran to and fro over the fields, many of them covered with the blood of their late riders." The Union troops managed to reach the heights after dark, where they saw Longstreet's campfires in the distance. This bit of information revealed where much of the Confederate Army was, if not where it was going. A thrust by Lee at Washington now seemed less likely. The Loudoun Valley scraps had cost each side cumulatively almost exactly the same butcher's bill as Brandy Station. The Union cavalry had gained little except to prove to their adversaries that the days of easy Confederate cavalry victories were gone.

The Army of the Potomac soon learned that Lee had already started to invade Pennsylvania. Hooker sent his men to pounding the roads north again, roads that led to the Potomac crossings and beyond. As the infantry marched, their cavalry searched south-central Maryland and Pennsylvania for Lee's invaders. While the Union cavalry fanned out, searching for their elusive foes,

Confederate cavalrymen captured at the battle of Aldie. They are mostly thin, wiry, small men. (Library of Congress)

Gregg's cavalry charges at the battle of Upperville. Notice the inscription "Blue Ridge Mts." in the background. (Library of Congress)

Lee's cavalry had separated into three groups. Lee had granted Stuart permission to ride around the Army of the Potomac with three brigades. Stuart may have felt the need to redeem his reputation, tarnished at Brandy Station and Upperville. He quickly found out that the Union Army was moving faster than expected, despite heat, high humidity and choking dust. He could not cut through it to return to Lee; nor could he tell Lee where he was; nor did Stuart know clearly where the main Confederate Army was. Stuart took nine days to circle back to the main army with the worn brigades of Hampton, "Fitz" Lee and Chambliss. Along the way the Confederate horsemen fought parts of Pleasonton's Corps at Hanover and Hunterstown in Pennsylvania. Stuart's command arrived in Gettysburg halfway through the battle. Lee might have fought differently, or not at all, if he had not been deprived of his "eyes and ears" by Stuart's absence. Stuart had left behind the brigades of Jones and Robertson, but Lee neglected to use them for scouting. The irregular cavalry brigades of Imboden and Jenkins mainly applied themselves to looting the bountiful Pennsylvania countryside.

General George Meade supplanted Hooker as commander of the Army of the Potomac on June 28. He immediately made several changes to his cavalry. Stahel's Division, newly transferred from the defenses of Washington, was rechristened the 3rd Division, Cavalry Corps, Army of the Potomac, and was assigned to Judson Kilpatrick. Meade agreed to Pleasonton's recommendation to promote three junior officers who had performed well at Brandy Station: Captains Wesley Merritt and Elon Farnsworth as well as Lieutenant George Custer became brigadier-generals. Even though they were dismissed at first as the "Boy Generals," they performed well. Kilpatrick gained Custer and Farnsworth for his division. Merritt took over the Regular Brigade in Buford's 1st Division. While he had never served in the cavalry, Meade could now appreciate how vital they were to his army during the drive into Pennsylvania. He now had close to 15,000 of them.

Three days later, the best of his cavalry commanders, John Buford, purchased three precious hours of time for the army by delaying Lee's infantry west of the town of Gettysburg. If Buford and his division had not given the Union infantry time to arrive and occupy key terrain, the battle of Gettysburg might well have been a Confederate victory. The three hours of fighting on July 1 by Buford's mainly dismounted troopers may have been the finest three hours of the Union cavalry during the war. Other accomplishments lay ahead

Buford's dismounted Union cavalry defending at Gettysburg. (Goss, Warren, *Recollections of a Private: A Story of the Army of the Potomac*, 1890)

at and after Gettysburg for the horsemen in blue. So much so that one of Stuart's staff officers observed that during the last two years of the war "no branch of the [Union army] contributed so much to the overthrow of Lee's army as the cavalry."

CAREERS AFTER GETTYSBURG

Alfred Pleasonton made the mistake of criticizing Meade's conduct at Gettysburg before the Congressional Joint Committee on the Conduct of the War. The new commander-in chief of the Union Armies in 1864, U. S. Grant, also wanted his own man, Sheridan, to command the Cavalry Corps of the Army of the Potomac. Pleasonton was thus sent west to command cavalry in Missouri, where he performed brilliantly. But Missouri was a stage with only a small audience and his deeds there were overshadowed by greater events elsewhere in 1864. With the reduction of the US Army after Appomattox, Pleasonton was offered a much lower rank and quit the military in disgust.

After the exhausting year of 1863, John Buford died of typhus in the army's winter camp at Brandy Station. Lincoln belatedly promoted him to major-general on his deathbed, the promotion backdated to the first day of Gettysburg. Thomas Devin served the Union faithfully until the end of the war. Alfred Duffie continued to be colorful. In late 1864, he so irritated his superiors that they relieved him of command of his division. Soon after that, the Confederates captured him and held him prisoner until near the end of the war. Later, he became US consul in Spain.

David Gregg resigned his commission a few months before the end of the war; no reason was given or was evident. Percy Wyndham joined Garibaldi again in 1866. Later he struggled to make money in South Asia and died when a balloon carrying him plunged to earth in Mandalay in 1879. Judson Kilpatrick led a large, disastrous cavalry raid against Richmond in early 1864 but turned back within sight of the city. He also infuriated Meade by criticizing him to Congress. He was sent to command cavalry under Sherman. "I know that Kilpatrick is a hell of a damned fool," Sherman supposedly confided, "but that's just the sort of man I want to command my cavalry." He commanded it through Georgia and the Carolinas and later behaved scandalously in the diplomatic corps; he never fulfilled his ambition to become President. David Russell was killed at the head of his division at Third Winchester in 1864. Adelbert Ames became a leader of the Radical Republicans in Congress after the war and a US Senator from Mississippi. He led troops during the Spanish-American War and was the last Civil War veteran of general rank to die, in 1933. Major Robert Morris, Jr., leader of the 6th Pennsylvania Cavalry in the bold attack at St. James Church and who was captured there, died a few weeks later in Libby Prison, Richmond. In late 1863, in an unusual move, Major Charles Whiting was thrown out of the army for "contemptuous and disrespectful" remarks about President Lincoln. Two aides of Pleasonton at Brandy Station traveled divergent paths. Ulric Dahlgren, by then a one-legged colonel, died on Kilpatrick's Richmond Raid. Orders found on his body created a major scandal because they seemed to encourage war atrocities. George Armstrong Custer became one of the best Union cavalry generals by the war's end. His life, though not his fame, came to an end along the Little Big Horn River in Montana, 11 years after the War for the Union.

Stuart received the second wound of his life, a mortal one, during a fight outside Richmond in May 1864. Robert E. Lee sadly recalled that "He never gave me a false piece of information." Lee put Wade Hampton in charge of the cavalry in the Army of Northern Virginia. Hampton led it with great skill despite the diminishing resources of the Confederacy. After the war Hampton became one of the great rebuilders of Southern society even though the war had come close to ruining him financially. He served as Governor of South Carolina and a US Senator. "Grumble" Jones continued his oil and water relationship with Stuart. In October 1863, a court martial ordered him reprimanded for behaving disrespectfully towards his superior. Transferred out of Lee's Army, Jones died in 1864 while leading a small Confederate army in his beloved Shenandoah Valley. "Rooney" Lee was captured by Union forces while recuperating from the wound received at Brandy Station. He was exchanged eight months later. Returning to his father's army, he became one of the great cavalry generals of the Confederacy. Beverly Robertson asked to be reassigned after the Gettysburg campaign, citing the weak strength of his brigade rather than his own weak performance. He was given a desk job in South Carolina for the rest of the war. Thomas Munford, whom Stuart roundly criticized for tardiness at Brandy Station, found this black mark blighted his career in the Confederate Army. Robert Franklin Beckham transferred to the Army of Tennessee in early 1864 to get a promotion and was mortally wounded at the battle of Franklin. Matthew Calbraith Butler, who lost his lower leg at Mountain Run, was back leading a brigade of South Carolina cavalry in the spring of 1864. Before long he became a divisional commander. He later served as a US Senator for three terms and a US general in the Spanish-American War.

THE BATTLEFIELD TODAY

The camp of the 18th Pennsylvania Cavalry near Stevensburg during the winter encampment of 1863/64. Note the log platforms built to keep the hoofs of the horses out of the mud. (Library of Congress)

The Army of the Potomac spent the winter of 1863/64 camped in Culpeper County and part of Fauquier; Brandy Station was the headquarters of this force of more than 120,000 men. The bucolic Virginia countryside where the battle was fought and an army camped changed little after the troops marched away and the trees grew back. In 1968, the county government created an airfield on the portion of the battlefield that lies east of the Beverly Ford Road, obliterating the woods held by Devin, the ground of Hampton's position and the Gee House site. Fortunately, the ground west of the road, including the site of St. James Church, the Gee House ridge, the ground over which the Two Sixes charged and much of the woods remains unspoiled. Also intact is Cunningham Ridge, the Green Farm, Yew Ridge and the remains of the contested stone wall between the Cunningham and Green farms. Part of Fleetwood Hill and its approach have been preserved. The Norfolk Southern Railroad now owns the Orange and Alexandria Railroad bed. The town of

ABOVE
A part of the camp of the headquarters of the Army of the Potomac on Fleetwood Hill during the winter encampment of 1863/64. (Library of Congress)

LEFT
The main depot at Brandy Station during the winter encampment of 1863/64. Note supply wagons with the 6th Corps' Greek Cross loading up. (Photo courtesy of the author)

Brandy Station is larger. Kelly's Ford and Stevensburg are easily accessible, but Beverly Ford is not. Modern Route 15/29 passes the town on ground where Wyndham charged. Many wartime buildings exist, but are privately owned, notably Auburn, Beauregard and the Wellford House. The Wiltshire House still stands.

In 1988, a Californian developer bought up much of the land where Buford fought and planned to build there a small city, including houses, office buildings and warehouses.

His plans were successfully thwarted by a coalition of local landowners, historians and preservationists, aided by a public interest law firm. This coalition formed the Brandy Station Foundation. After the developer sold a large part of his land to an entrepreneur who planned a Formula One racetrack, the foundation defeated this new project. The coalition also persuaded a private land trust with a national base called the Association for

the Preservation of Civil War Sites to purchase over 700 acres of threatened battlefield. The successor organization to the APCWS, called the Civil War Preservation Trust—now located in Washington, DC—added to the preserved acreage. Today about 1,000 acres are saved, including nearly 30 acres by the Brandy Station Foundation. The CWPT has installed 14 interpretive signs, trails, and has driving tours sketched out.

The place to start any tour of Brandy Station is the Graffiti House in Brandy Station (so called because Civil War soldiers left names and drawings

on its plaster walls). This headquarters of the non-profit Brandy Station Foundation has exhibits, maps, guided tours, books, and of course, graffiti.

There are no granite or marble monuments to valor, dedication or comradeship at Brandy Station, except one small, easily overlooked one on Fleetwood Hill. The woods and streams, hills and meadows of the battlefield, preserved through the hard work and dedication of the Civil War Preservation Trust and the Brandy Station Foundation, are the real monuments at Brandy Station.

Part of the land saved for this and future generations by the Civil War Preservation Trust. The view is south from Buford's Knoll, across Ruffin's Run. The distant woods once held the bivouac of Beckham's artillery battalion. (Photo by Peggy Beattie)

FURTHER READING

For many years after the events, there was no history of the battle of Brandy Station. In 1959, Fairfax Downey wrote *Clash of Cavalry: the Battle of Brandy Station* (New York: David McKay Company, Inc., 1959). While well written, only half of the slim book is devoted to the battle, the rest is information on how cavalry functioned. Much better and taking advantage of much new material is Joseph W. McKinney, *Brandy Station, Virginia, June 9, 1863: the Largest Cavalry Battle of the Civil War* (Jefferson, NC/London: McFarland & Company, Inc, Publishers, 2006).

The best one-volume in the copious library of books on Gettysburg is the brilliantly written *Gettysburg* (Boston/New York: Houghton Mifflin Company, 2003) by Stephen W. Sears. It covers the period from Brandy Station until Lee returns to Virginia after Gettysburg. More focused on the cavalry during that campaign is Edward G. Longacre's *The Cavalry at Gettysburg: a Tactical Study of Mounted Operations during the Civil War's Pivotal Campaign. 9 June–14 July 1863* (Rutherford, New Jersey: Fairleigh Dickenson University Press, 1986).

A serious student should use the classic *The War of the Rebellion: a Compilation of the Official Records of the Union and Confederate Armies, 70 vols in 128, and Atlas* (Washington, DC, Government Printing Office, 1880–1901), published by the United States War Department, and the more recent *Supplement to the Official Records* 100 vols (Wilmington, NC: Broadfoot Publishing Company, 1994–2000). They contain many orders and after-action reports on Brandy Station. Also useful for first-person accounts is *Annals of the War, Written by Leading Participants North and South*, a series of columns the Philadelphia Weekly Times published in the 1870s. I used the edition published by the Blue and Grey Press of Edison, New Jersey, in 1996. Very useful were William W. Blackford's *War Years with Jeb Stuart* (New York: Charles Scribner's Sons, 1945) and Henry B. McClellan's *The Life and Campaigns of Maj. Gen. J.E.B. Stuart, Commander of the Cavalry of the Army of Northern Virginia* (Boston: Houghton, Mifflin & Co., 1885).

For material on the development of the cavalry during the Civil War, see Stephen Z. Starr, *The Union Cavalry in the Civil War* 3 vols. (Baton Rouge: Louisiana State University Press, 1979–85) and Edward G. Longacre's two books: *Lincoln's Cavalrymen: a History of the Mounted Forces of the Army of the Potomac* (Mechanicsburg, Pennsylvania: Stackpole Books, 2000) and *Lee's Cavalrymen: a History of the Mounted Forces of the Army of Northern Virginia* (Mechanicsburg, Pennsylvania: Stackpole Books, 2002). The Osprey books, *Union Cavalryman* (Warrior 13) and *Confederate Cavalryman* (Warrior 54) are sound.

The best overview of its subject is Jack Coggins's *Arms and Equipment of the Civil War* (Wilmington, NC: Broadfoot Publishing Company, 1990). First published in 1962, it is a well-written masterpiece that also discusses tactics briefly. Paddy Griffith's *Battle in the Civil War* (Mansfield, England: Field Books. 1986) is a brilliant survey with magnificent illustrations. Brent Nosworthy's *The Bloody Crucible of Courage: Fighting Methods and Combat Experience of the Civil War* (New York: Carroll and Graf Publishers, 2003) is provocative.

INDEX